Praise for *The Art of Change Leadership*

"*The Art of Change Leadership: Driving Transformation in a Fast-Paced World*" by Cheryl Cran provides real-time ideas, strategies, and creative solutions for leaders to help drive innovation and change in the workplace."

> —Tony Hsieh, NY *Times* bestselling author of
> *Delivering Happiness* and CEO of Zappos.com

"In our rapid paced, information overloaded, and energy-deprived world, understanding the dynamics of change and human performance are essential leadership skills.

"In her fifth book, business change expert Cheryl Cran shares her much needed wisdom on how to apply your unique skills and stay ahead of the curve by leaping to (r)evolutionary change leadership!"

> —Dr. Donald Epstein, founder of Epstein Institute;
> author, *Energetics of Extraordinary*

"The capacity to change is the new competitive advantage for businesses and individuals. Cheryl Cran powerfully shows how to be a change champion while leading others to do the same."

> —John Izzo, author of *Stepping Up & Awakening Corporate Soul*

"Buy this book! *The Art of Change Leadership: Driving Transformation in a Fast Paced World* provides a roadmap for leaders and their teams to become more resilient, more agile, and more innovative, and as a result, more profitable. This book details ideas, strategies, and revolutionary plans to help your organization be *the* industry leader and gain a competitive advantage."

> —Colleen Francis, president of Engage Selling and author of
> *Nonstop Sales Boom*

"Cheryl Cran's book, *The Art of Change Leadership: Driving Transformation In a Fast-Paced World* is a *must* read!

"The fast pace of change is impacting all industries and this book provides a road map to navigate and 'win.'"

> —Peter Legge, CEO of Canada Wide Media, author of
> *The Runway of Life*

"Cheryl Cran's new book focuses on the ultimate tipping point of change, technology, and people, with a unique understanding of how each organizational member must assume full responsibility for not only appreciating this vital interface, but also leading the way—regardless of where in the traditional hierarchy that member happens to reside. Cheryl also provides numerous assessments and exercises to help members discover their special gifts for successfully leading the transformation process in their organization."

—**Ralph H. Kilmann, PhD, author of *Quantum Organizations* and**
The Courageous Mosaic: *Awakening Society, Systems, and Souls*

"*The Art of Change Leadership: Driving Transformation In a Fast-Paced World* is a seminal work that bridges the often-ignored gap between process and people during change. A real-time, pragmatic blend of the 'what' and 'how,' this book should be part of every leader's toolkit who wants to not only accelerate change, drive organizational agility, and reap the benefits of genuine collaboration but also to personally thrive and develop continuously."

—**Simon Horan, Global Change Management training director, UK**

"Outstanding change leadership is more vital today than perhaps any other time in history. No matter if you were born a leader or acquired the role of leadership, it's essential to know *how* to lead change. Discover for yourself not only what it takes to be a great change leader but how to be a great change leader. If you have the desire to be a master leader of change, Cheryl's new book is a must read."

—**Dr. Richard Kaye, regional director of CEO Space**

The ~~Art~~ of
Art

~~Change~~
Change

~~Leadership~~
Leadership

The ~~Art~~ of

~~Change~~

~~Leadership~~ Leadership

Driving Transformation In a Fast-Paced World

Cheryl Cran

WILEY

Published by John Wiley & Sons, Inc., Hoboken, New Jersey
Published simultaneously in Canada

For general information about our other products and services, please contact our Customer Care Department within the United States at (800) 762-2974, outside the United States at (317) 572-3993 or fax (317) 572-4002.

Wiley publishes in a variety of print and electronic formats and by print-on-demand. Some material included with standard print versions of this book may not be included in e-books or in print-on-demand. If this book refers to media such as a CD or DVD that is not included in the version you purchased, you may download this material at http://booksupport.wiley.com. For more information about Wiley products, visit www.wiley.com.

Library of Congress Cataloging-in-Publication Data:

Cran, Cheryl, 1963-
 The art of change leadership : driving transformation in a fast-paced world / Cheryl Cran.
   pages cm
 Includes index.
 ISBN 978-1-119-12475-7 (hardback) 978-1-119-12477-1 (ePDF) 978-1-119-12476-4 (epub)
 1. Organizational change. 2. Leadership. I. Title.
 HD58.8.C717 2015
 658.4′ 092–dc23
                         2015020389

Cover design: Michael J. Freeland

Printed in the United States of America

10 9 8 7 6 5 4 3 2 1

This book is dedicated to my biggest fan and supporter, Reg Cran, who has unfailingly been there throughout all of the many changes and transformations. Here's to the future and many more!

CONTENTS

PREFACE

The Art of Change Leadership—Driving Transformation in a Fast-Paced World

The only thing that is constant is change.

—Heraclitus

How has your life changed in the past five years?
How has your workplace changed in the past five years?

Collectively there has been more change in the past five years than previous generations experienced in a lifetime!

In the spring of 2010 my book, *101 Ways to Make Generations X, Y and Zoomers Happy at Work,* was published. It was based on client research with dozens of organizations in North America who were asking, "What is with the younger generations?" and, at that time, the generations' impact was seen as one of the biggest forces of change. My generations research and work with clients produced significant transformations as they applied to reorganizing, elevating leadership capability, and enhancing cultural renewal and business growth.

In 2012 my next book released was the popular *Leadership Mastery in the Digital Age,* which was based on the fact that it was *not* just the generations that were causing massive change in organizations; rather, it was in a big way the technological revolution. Technology was and is creating massive upheaval. It continues to evolve quickly and this impacts employees' abilities to keep up and provide speedy customer delivery. Technology has given customers access to information and technology has a major impact on increasing global competition.

I have worked with hundreds of clients globally in diverse industries such as technology, insurance, finance, manufacturing, healthcare, and more, and I have helped leaders to integrate the change-cycle model into their strategy to drive transformation. Thus, this book was born.

You might be asking, why this book and why now?

In this book I build on the strategies and virtues of the two previous books and provide a holistic plan to lead change and drive transformation in a fast-paced world. I use the word *holistic* to expand the perceptions around change beyond how it is currently viewed. Many leaders and organizations hear the word *change* and they balk because it implies that what they are doing right now isn't working. Shifting the word to *transformation* helps and yet there are many who are still afraid of the implications of change with fears such as "something has to go" (me/my job/my autonomy/my identity/my company).

A holistic approach to change and transformation comes from the positive assumption that what you have done as a leader and as an organization and what you are currently doing have been and are *already successful.* In addition, there is a realization that you must be *open* and *build* on the successes of the past; you must include all stakeholders in the new vision/direction of what is possible; and, rather than focus on *eliminate* or *lose,* you focus on reinventing, re-creating, and reorganizing the entire system. The holistic approach is inclusive and *all* is seen as an ally: all people, all systems, all products, all customers, and you focus on including *all* while building renewed strategies and approaches.

My mission is to massively shift the view and approach to transformation away from "something or someone has to lose" and toward "everyone has something to gain." This book is not about change management; it is about creating organizational cultures with change leaders.

This book progresses from the I to the we and begins with the compelling reasons that your change leadership and transformation abilities are needed right now. It moves through the concept that only by adding value and sharing value can we authentically and abundantly seek to create changes that benefit the greater system (you, your team, the company, your industry, and the world).

I present research and information that confirms that there are tools that include mindfulness and emotional intelligence that can speed the pace of individual and collective transformation.

Clarification is given on the difference between a change manager and a change leader and why an integration of the skills of each is needed in this rapidly changing era.

The subject of technology appears throughout the book and indicates the massive opportunity to leverage existing technology knowledge within organizations in order to speed up the rate of innovation.

I share holistic thought leaders' overviews of the power of harnessing the energy of people to lead change and to empower those same people to become more effective leaders of change.

The change-cycle model is examined and is used as a reference tool for you to check yourself as a change leader, where you are in the cycle, and as a check-up tool for your organization.

I review the current and up-to-date research on the generations as it relates to the global changes affecting business today and ideas on how to integrate the strengths of *all* the generations to drive transformation.

The three-step change model simplifies the *key* areas of leading change and provides a guideline for project management of change initiatives.

Last, a leadership survey of over 200 leaders from middle management to C-suite provides further supporting data and insight to the changes affecting organizations, the challenges, and the opportunities for transforming the current workplace into the workplace of the future—today!

As always, it is my clients who have inspired this book. I have tremendous respect and admiration for the leaders I work with, for their courage and their drive toward transformation—and some of their stories are included.

May 2015   Cheryl Cran

ACKNOWLEDGMENTS

A book is a collaboration. There is an author's name on the front but there are many people involved who support the process and make it all happen.

I am grateful to the entire team at John Wiley & Sons for their help in polishing the jewel. I would also like to acknowledge the speakers' bureaus that partner with me to bring my change leadership and future of work research to their clients. To *all* my clients who are living testaments to the power of the strategies in this book: I am honored to work with you.

I offer a loving shout-out to my partner/friend/husband, Reg Cran, who is my biggest fan and supporter of all my books and work. There is no way I could have done any of the work I love to do without his ongoing cheerleading. I must also mention my father Dave Chouinard who was the master of change, was way ahead of his time as an entrepreneur, and influenced me from a young age to be agile, resilient, and able to lead change.

The ~~Art~~ of
Art

~~Change~~
Change

~~Leadership~~
Leadership

Why Do Organizations Need Change Leaders?

The rate of change is not going to slow down anytime soon.
If anything, competition in most industries will probably
speed up even more in the next few decades.

—John Kotter

The future workplace is now—is your organization
ready?

Are you ready?

We need change leaders now because the fast pace of change
has made it an imperative. Why?

Because fast change means there is a need for people to
adapt quickly. The truth is that change involves human beings
who must be willing to move away from the familiar and move
toward the unknown and embrace it.

The art of change leadership is to understand the fundamental of change from a human point of view. When we as change
leaders consistently use strategies to improve our own approach
to change and then share those strategies with those we lead,
then we can effectively create sustainable organizational change.
That's the goal of this book, to provide the human (feelings,
thoughts, and behaviors) and the structural (steps to be taken)

strategies as well as the behaviors (action/execution) that will drive transformation in our fast paced world.

In the past 10 years, there have been massive changes. The Conference Board surveyed 1,020 global chief executive officers (CEOs) in 2014 and asked them to rank their top business challenges. *Human capital, customer relationships, innovation, operational excellence,* and *corporate brand and reputation* emerged as the top five challenges. Although these challenges may have been similar a decade ago, at the core of these challenges is the underlying theme—the need to change the solutions. The solutions to the top five challenges are not the same that would have been applied even a year or so ago. The challenges require new solutions, which in turn requires change.

Human capital is the biggest issue keeping many CEOs up at night—it used to be that employees would find a career in an industry, remain in that industry for 20-some years, and then retire. My, how things have changed! Now, employers are faced with the reality of changing employee attitudes about work and life. The increase of technological innovation has created greater access for employees to educate themselves, to seek out other opportunities, and to seek more meaningful and impactful work. Generations of workers are finding that there is value in working smarter not harder and having fun at work. The changes needed to master the human capital challenge include having change leaders who can drive transformation in the fast paced and fast changing workplace reality. Imagine organizations that have recognized the need to build the future workplace today and to prepare their leaders for ongoing and rapid change. Imagine organizations having leaders who are able to inspire, share knowledge, and provide resources to their teams while creating a work environment that is open, creative, collaborative, and focused on transformational experiences for the employees and the clients.

The leadership skills that have been used for the past decade are not the skills that are going to create next level growth or expansion for organizations. We need change leaders with upgraded operating systems to inspire and create new approaches, new processes, and new ways of connecting to create an organization with happy employees.

Customers have become right-now consumers who want what they want and they want it *now*—not yesterday! Amazon Prime and its two-day delivery is still not fast enough for some of the drone-loving customers who want their deliveries *today*. Years ago the customer could wait. I remember a situation when I worked in banking: I was right out of high school and was promoted from bank teller to side-counter customer service. This was in the 1980s when customer service was not a "thing" and a customer came to the side counter and I jumped up ready to serve him. My co-worker who had been in customer service for years yanked me back down and said, "Don't get up so quickly or the customers will always expect us to jump." I was in my teens at the time and remember thinking how silly that was. Fast forward to today and the customer IS king or queen and drives all solutions from the business perspective and also from the individual consumer perspective. In fact, I find that customer expectation of stellar service has gone up so high that there is a pervasive culture of never satisfied customers out there. So what does that mean for organizations? It means that the continued and increasing demands from customers are creating the need for adaptable and customized solutions. The ability to provide creative and innovative customer care requires a change of mind-set around what constitutes good service and a change in customer delivery processes. We need change leaders to transform customer processes.

Innovation is something that keeps many CEOs up at night as he or she struggles with staying one step ahead of the competition. An innovative culture requires teams of people to be thinking in new ways that are continually focused on creative solutions. Leaders and employees who may have been working in a culture in which new ideas were not valued are finding the new economy and new workplace demands creativity and innovation mindsets. The approaches, strategies, and processes all need to change in order to shift to a culture of innovation. We need change leaders to focus and create environments and structures that support innovation and creativity. Organizational executives need to value new ideas and create opportunities for employees to share ideas, to openly spend time creating, and to be rewarded for innovative product ideas, customer service improvement ideas, employee engagement ideas, and more. Many organizations are establishing forums and labs for innovation; for example AT&T and the AT&T Foundry™ innovation centers are fast-paced and collaborative environments. AT&T and technology providers work in the AT&T Foundry to deliver applications and services to customers more quickly than ever before.

The AT&T Foundry works in projects combining business, design, and technical resources. Since its launch in 2011, the AT&T Foundry has started more than 200 projects and deployed dozens of new products and services. Projects focus on areas of significant business or technology interest and typically involve external start-ups, innovators, entrepreneurs, academics, and inventors. Projects are organized in short sprints designed to determine success or failure quickly.

Another area that is undergoing massive change approaches is the operational excellence of the organization overall. Many organizations have policies and procedures that were established decades ago and that may or may not have relevance to today's business reality. When our team conducts organizational assessments with our consulting clients one of the questions asked is, "What are the policies and procedures you have in place that are not serving your actual objectives?" A company may state that their objective is for absolute customer satisfaction and yet the operations and processes hinder that same objective.

For example a company that has been in business for over 30 years or more may have had a policy to give absolutely no refunds to the customer, and today that same company has a direct competitor who does provide refunds for the same product. Does the policy need to change? That may seem like a stupid question and yet there are many organizations in which the operations and methods have not been changed, updated, or modified to meet the current customer or employee reality. We need change leaders in operations to lead operational excellence and to help drive transformation in the organization.

The corporate brand and reputation focus from the survey mentioned earlier is a key area for company success in the next few years. It used to be that you could manage brand and reputation by "spinning" content to ensure the best possible image was put forward. Now with social media and outspoken customers a brand slipup can go viral in seconds. Larger corporations have had social media staff for the past five years focus on brand and reputation management by focusing on Twitter feeds, YouTube video comments, and more. In addition, individuals within companies are recognizing the need and value to have a personal brand to promote skills for new jobs, for promotion opportunities, and more. I read recently that new parents are buying URLs for their babies either prior to birth or right after birth to ensure brand protection. The need for rapid adaptation to the brand and reputation challenge is an imperative. We need leaders of change to lead everyone within the company to be brand advocates, to leverage all channels of strategic brand promotion, and to see the interconnection of company brand with each individual's representation of the brand.

A NEED FOR BREAKTHROUGH TRANSFORMATION

All the items discussed here provide insight into the areas that CEOs will be focused on in the next few years. However, there are new trends that are shaping the future of work and that have to be factored in when looking at driving transformation in the workplace.

The trends that are impacting business today are increasing technological innovation, Generation Y impact on the workplace, and cloud computing.

Technological Innovation

Let's look at the impact of technological innovation: 10 years ago if someone told you that you would share most of your life both private and personal for the world to read, watch, and hear, you would have said they were nuts. We now live in a 24/7 information-packed reality where we can find out virtually anything we want about anyone at any time. Who would have thought that we would be living more public lives, building online communities, sharing photos, videos, and personal stories, communicating, collaborating, and accessing information all through the use of technology? It is the impact of technology that is radically changing the way we live and work, and organizations must be adapting to the technological revolution that is upon us. The need for organizations and their leaders to guide the change of technological transformation is absolutely essential. Eric Qualman, the creator of *Social Media Revolution* videos, states a statistic that in the next few years we will not have a Fortune 500; rather, we will have a Fortune 100. That is, the rapidity with which technology is impacting business and the ability of businesses to respond will determine whether the company will still be relevant in the next few years.

The organizations that are focused on technological transformation are well positioned to be successful and relevant. Often when I speak to groups of traditional organizations (those who have been in business for over 30 years or more) I notice that there is an obvious opportunity for many of these companies. The obvious opportunity is to get everyone in the company on board with the technological solutions that can be utilized. I was facilitating an executive retreat with a company that had been in the telephone business for over 20 years and now wanted to rebrand to let its customers know that they were now a technology company. When we were going through the SWOT (strengths, weaknesses, opportunities, threats) analysis with the executive team, the vice president of sales stated that she did not need to know the technology because her team had full knowledge of it. I stopped and looked directly at the VP of sales and then the CEO and said nothing. I waited for the CEO to say something to the VP and then I said, "Let me get this straight. You are rebranding to be a technology firm and yet *you* don't need to know the new technology?" The room was silent. Then I went on to say, "In the past it is true that a leader did not need to know the technicalities of the work that the team members did, but in today's reality the leaders *must* know as much as they possibly can about the technology in order to have relevance with the team." The CEO had been accepting the approach of the VP of sales because he was not willing to engage in a dialogue with her about how she needed to step up and be more proactive in her role and to learn as much as she could about the technology. This company had a need for breakthrough transformation in order to achieve the objective of being a technology firm rather than a telephone firm. The attitudes and the behaviors of the executives needed to fundamentally change in order to transform and drive business forward. I am happy to say that as a result of that two-day retreat, the company went on with the rebrand and a new commitment to training and upgrading of leadership skills to ensure the focus remained on transformation and making positive change.

Generation Y

The Generation Y impact is a profound change that I identified and that I have helped clients with over the past five years. When I wrote my book, *101 Ways to Make Generations X, Y and Zoomers Happy at Work* in 2010 it was as a result of clients telling me that they were being majorly challenged by this new younger demographic who was in the workforce.

By 2020, Generation Ys are expected to make up around 50 percent of the workforce; by 2025 this number is projected to be 75 percent. Yes Generation Ys bring new approaches, innovations, unique values, and ways of working, *and* they are going to be the dominant demographic in the workplace, which means what they want will rule. This is a generation that has technological intelligence and innateness and that is focused on working smarter with the use of technology rather than *harder* (aka longer hours).

Many Generation Ys will live at home until the average age of 35; they are willing to live at home longer until they find a company that they truly want to work for. Gen Y are either staying home longer until they find work they love or they are working at what they want but it doesn't quite pay enough for them to move out. The implication for organizations is that they must shift from creating an environment in which they assume people *need* to work to one in which people *want* to work.

We need to transform the workplace and the culture to include the viewpoints and ideas of Generation Y and to be engaging for all of the generations. Generation Ys are not the reason companies need to transform; the reason for the transformation imperative is technology, and Generation Y happens to be the generation infiltrating the workplace that has been born with technology as a part of their life since birth. Generation X or Baby Boomer parents taught Generation Ys to do what they love, to ask for what they want, and that life is too short to be in one job for life. Because of this, Generation Ys show up at work and want the workplace to segue to their lives; they want it to be fun, to be collegial, to be creative, and to have the ability to enjoy life while having a career. The art of change leadership includes the ability to adapt to the Generation Y influence and to incorporate their ideas as well as their creative solutions for driving transformation forward.

Cloud Computing

The other trend that is impacting the need for transformation is cloud computing. Big data, the cloud, robots, real time, video, collaboration tools, and open-source platforms are changing everything. The cloud puts the power of technology in the hands of employees. Robotics is forcing us to rethink the jobs that humans can and should do. Recently, I was a keynote speaker for the American Manufacturing Excellence conference on finding and keeping good people, and robotics was a big item of focus because many mundane and repetitive tasks in the manufacturing industry are being replaced with robotics. Interestingly a 2015 statistic by Fortune 500 magazine says that 82% of CEOs of the biggest companies plan to employ more people two years from now than they do today even with robotics entering the workplace. The change of bringing on robotics is in response to one of the biggest challenges for many traditional industries, namely finding talented new people, and many Generation Ys are happy to do jobs that involve technology such as operating robots and not so happy doing jobs of repetitive labor (the jobs that robots do).

Big data is also giving us insights into the metrics of how we work and how customers interact with us. Collaboration tools give us the ability to connect people and information together anywhere, anytime, and on any device. Data collection as a focus has shifted into data action–leveraging information from data mining to improve customer deliverables and business results.

Business agility has become the primary advantage being delivered by the cloud, says a new survey by Harvard Business Review Analytic Services of 527 *Harvard Business Review (HBR)* readers in large and midsize organizations. Business agility is the main objective for adopting cloud computing, with nearly a third of respondents (32 percent) saying it was their primary reason for pursuing the cloud. This was followed by increased innovation (14 percent), lower costs (14 percent), and the ability to scale up and down in response to variations in business demand (13 percent). So you can see the need for breakthrough transformation in this fast-paced and changing world. The human requirement is for all of us to master the art of change leadership. This requires the ability to be responsive and quickly adaptive to change and to have the mental agility and the emotional agility to lead people to the exciting future of business that lies ahead.

THE INCREASING NEED FOR INNOVATION AND SPEED

In addition to the need for breakthrough and transformation, there is the ongoing reality of the speed of change and the need for rapid innovation. In the example of the AT&T Foundry a structure was created to focus on innovation as a main driver for the business. There is an opportunity for an organization of any size to create its own innovation hub. There are innovation hubs available for start-up companies, but what if existing companies created their own innovation hubs similar to AT&T's. An example of an innovation incubator is Innovation HUB—Florida Innovation HUB at the University of Florida. The mission of the Innovation HUB is as follows:

> The Florida Innovation Hub was created to serve as catalyst for start-up companies whose technologies emanated from laboratories at the University of Florida and throughout the state. Our mission is to provide them with the infrastructure, logistics, and resources needed to get up and running effectively and efficiently. In doing so, the Innovation Hub hopes to help those companies and others bring research discoveries to the marketplace, creating additional jobs for Floridians.

The Florida Innovation HUB is modeled after successful entrepreneurial-focused commercialization centers. According to the National Business Incubation Association (NBIA), companies that graduate from a business incubator create jobs, revitalize neighborhoods and commercialize new technologies, thus strengthening local, regional, and national economies. Historically, NBIA member incubators have reported that 87 percent of all firms that have graduated from their incubators are still in business.

What is great about innovation centers such as the Florida HUB is that it provides a format for continual research and innovation. Many organizations say they want to be innovative and speedy and yet they have not created a format or environment for both of these things to be focused on. We need future focused change leaders who will not only question whether they have processes aligned with what the company and executives say they want to create but who will actually lead the change to create the solutions and the infrastructures to ensure that innovation is a consistent focus. The manufacturing industry has recognized the need for innovation hubs; in 2014, three Manufacturing Innovation Institutes were announced, each geared toward a particular field of manufacturing development and funded in a similar fashion. At North Carolina State University at Raleigh, an innovation hub known as the Next Generation Power Electronics National Manufacturing Innovation Institute was launched in January 2014 and tasked with improving energy efficiency. N.C. State and its partners will tackle the broad challenge by advancing the technology and production of special power-oriented semiconductors to improve efficiency in applications ranging from electronic devices to electric vehicles.

Innovation today is not innovation of the past. In the past, innovation was led by the senior leaders who would then report back to the employees about the innovations that were going to take place. Today, innovation requires open-source. Think Tesla and this excerpt from a June 12, 2014 blog post from Elon Musk on the philosophy of sharing for the sake of innovation:

> **Excerpt from *All Our Patents Belong to You***
> **Elon Musk, CEO, June 12, 2014**
> If we clear a path to the creation of compelling electric vehicles, but then lay intellectual property landmines behind us to inhibit others, we are acting in a manner contrary to that goal. Tesla will not initiate patent lawsuits against anyone who, in good faith, wants to use our technology.

Elon Musk is an example of a change leader who is focused on the bigger picture of innovation and speed; his overwhelming objective is to have more electric cars a reality sooner than later.

So what if we applied Tesla's approach to innovation in our companies today? Innovation as a collaborative approach not only solves the transformation dilemma, it also creates greater engagement for all employees within the company. In order to create speedy innovation, it takes more than a few people; it takes a village. Steve Jobs acknowledged that he had creative vision and he was quick to state that he had a team of talented developers and creators that worked together and in a dynamic way that encouraged sharing ideas, challenging the ideas in a healthy way, and then sharing the innovation as quickly as they could to the market.

In fact, it is speedy innovation that keeps Apple as one of the world's top performing organizations. No sooner do they release a new version of the iPhone, they are consistently and constantly creating new products with new features that are right on target with the consumer needs. In fact, one of Apple's many successful business approaches is anticipating what the customer wants before he or she even knows they want it.

Innovation and speed is not limited to technology. You and I both know that technology needs humans to operate it (well, at least so far!). As change leaders who drive transformation, we as humans need to increase our speed of thinking, of linking unknown things together, of connecting with each other in helpful and productive ways, and in adding value to employees and customers. How? There will be more about that later on in the chapters that follow.

WHO IS RESPONSIBLE FOR LEADING CHANGE?

I know it's an obvious question, and yet, is it?

You may already inherently know that *you* are responsible for leading change, you are the one reading this book, you are the one who is a leader either with the title or without the title in your workplace. It is my philosophy that *everyone* is a leader! Being a leader of change is very different than being a reactor to change. One drives success forward, the other resists the fast pace of change and slows down progress. Do me a favor and right now pick up a pen or use your personal device with a writing app and write your name using your opposite hand. Now, if you are ambidextrous, you have an advantage, but must of us are not. Notice that the writing is not as legible, smooth, or pretty as when you write with your dominant hand? Why?

Because we use our dominant hand to write, writing with our dominant hand has become an unconscious competency we just do. This is how many people respond to change: he or she has a way of reacting to change and that way either creates progress or it hinders it.

If you were to practice writing with your nondominant hand for about 30 to 90 days, you would be able to write more competently with your opposite hand and you would be able to increase your skill set to write with either hand you chose to use. The same is true for change.

If you focus on being more responsive, flexible, open, and creative for a minimum of 30 days you will begin to create a new level of unconscious competency.

So if *you* are responsible for being a leader of change, what is it going to take for you to be a master leader of change?

First, it takes desire; do you *want* to be more responsive, more creative, more engaging, and create more dynamic results?

Next, it takes commitment; are you willing to do what it takes to create the next level of flexibility and adaptability knowing that it will create more excitement and energy for yourself as well as for those you influence?

Last, it takes a calling; do you know that your legacy, the reason you are here is to make a lasting impact with how you show up and with how you inspire and motivate others to navigate these times of fast-paced change?

If you answered yes to these three questions, then you have answered what Joseph Campbell calls the heroes' journey: the desire to be a master of change leadership and to make an even bigger impact on the world than you already have.

The other answer to who is responsible for change leadership is *everyone*.

As a change leadership expert, I have found that, for many people, change is hard. Many people say they want to change and they make an effort and then inevitably they fall back to the previous way of doing things.

Psychologically change can be overwhelming. This is because we are wired for fight or flight. These reactions are helpful when we are in a life or death situation but not so helpful when we want to navigate change with speed and innovation!

Depending on personality and the amount of change someone has had in his or her life and work they may view change as a threat or as an opportunity. As a leader of change, the art of change leadership is to better understand how people can succeed at it and to inspire them to move with it.

I often tell my clients and audiences that, to be a successful leader today, we must all become better psychologists to better understand why people might be resistant to a specific direction and to understand to a deeper level how to shift them to be a part of the change.

Leaders must also better understand behavioral economics— the study of how human thought and behavior affect decisions provides us with clues for why creating lasting change is so difficult. Factors such as status quo bias (a preference for keeping things the same) and loss aversion (the tendency to prefer avoiding pain more strongly than acquiring progress) interact to stack the odds against employees acting very differently for very long.

Gallup conducted a study of effective change management using the Change Management Index, and found that managers in the top quartile engaged 77 percent of their employees on average. Managers in the bottom quartile engaged only 1 percent of their employees on average, and 54 percent of their employees were actively disengaged. Even when an organization's leaders advocate for change, when more than half of the employees on a given team do not participate, it's difficult to make that change happen.

Talented managers who engage their teams and assist their employees to see how their work connects to the vision for the future are key to every successful change approach. Talented managers deliver daily focus to keep employees moving in the change direction rather than waiting for annual performance reviews to help them correct their course. In these times of fast change, we use technology to be a part of our tools for keeping everyone focused on the new change direction. A great example of this is real-time performance tools that recognize and reward people for the activities we want to establish as the new norm. Companies like www.work.com and https://www.7geese.com/welcome/ provide instant feedback through texting, e-mail or group messaging to employees when they are exhibiting the actions aligned with the desired behaviors that are aligned with the change direction of the company. Tools like this increase the speed of feedback as well as reinforcing desired behaviors by those in the company.

SO WHY DO ORGANIZATIONS NEED CHANGE LEADERS?

We need change leaders because we are living and working in times of major transformation. We must have change leaders because change leaders are transformers helping to drive innovation forward. We need change leaders because change is challenging and we need change leaders to model how to thrive and innovate and create positive outcomes.

In the next chapter, we consider why you and why now, which will include a few quizzes and self-assessment tools to help you get clear on your strengths as a change leader and your areas for development. There will also be an opportunity to practice what you learn and to set a personal plan for 30, 60, and 90 days so that you can further enhance your unconscious competency as a change leader.

2

Fast Changing World Needs
Leaders Like You

If not you, who? If not now, when?

—Hillel

Cultures can be transformed. Leadership teams can and do evolve the mind-sets within a culture. Individuals, teams, and entire companies can adapt and prepare for the future. By studying what to change and how to do it, each learns to expand the mind in order to solve bigger challenges.

How is this accomplished? It is accomplished with exceptional leadership, with immense energy, and with tremendous skill and a willingness to lead self and others through change and to drive transformation forward.

Organizations that know they need to adapt during turbulent times—like now—cannot make change happen through purely technical approaches or by continually restructuring. Restructuring of the past has been simply changing departments and silos and moving people around or downsizing without any fundamental change to the leadership focus on people, the core goals and values that the company espouses. It is change for change's sake, which is not what we are talking about in this book. All people within the company must commit to the transformational change being described in this book to a new way of being and doing business that requires new skills and new attitudes. Organizations need a new kind of leadership capability to reframe issues, reinterpret situations, and transform operations.

An IBM study of CEOs in 2012 stated that one of the three areas that were of prime focus for the next decade was creating shared value for employees and clients.

ADDING VALUE—A CHANGE LEADER APPROACH

Organizations that are continuously looking to add value are able to adapt and flex to the market reality of client demands as well as apply the add value concept to the employees within the organization. Some examples of companies that look to continuously add value include Apple, Porsche, and Disney to name a few. The focus for all three of these companies is how to improve the customer experience while also providing added value to the people who work for the brand. According to an article in the *Wall Street Journal* in 2012, Apple CEO Tim Cook brought added value to the employees in the form of perks.

These perks, according to the article, included discounts on Apple products, a program that matches employees' personal charitable contributions up to a set amount, and "Blue Sky," which gives small groups of employees a dedicated amount of time to spend on their favorite engineering projects. Cook has taken other steps to make Apple's workforce feel more valued—such as praising employees at public events and trying harder to retain individuals who get outside job offers.

Google is another example of a company that at its core is an innovation culture and recognizes the need to add value to the employees in order to increase commitment to the fast pace of work and innovation.

Google's approach has often been to be an idea-generator company: the more ideas the better. Leaders at Google focus on being an incubation center for great ideas, and, rather than worry about losing good people (fear), they are more focused on being a place known for generating ongoing great ideas (progress). As a result of this type of added-value approach to culture, Google is one of the most desired places to work.

The company wants to be known as a place where really smart people are doing innovative things. The leadership at Google has developed leadership mastery programs that are based on what the top-performing leaders at Google do, and those leadership behaviors have formed the leadership training for all leaders at Google. They recognize that, by building leadership capability, they are able to sustain being a culture of fast-paced change and innovation ability.

Building leadership capability is a keystone of the art of change leadership within an organization. Organizations that focus on educating and building leadership skills as a consistent focus are able to not only set vision for change but also to execute it because of the focus on developing the leaders' and teams' skill sets.

The Walt Disney Company provides a great example in the book, *Disney U—How Disney University Develops the World's Most Engaged, Loyal and Customer-Centric Employees*. Doug Lipp writes about the leadership of Van France, the founder of Disney University, as an example of how Disney culture aims to add value to its employees, as well as to its customers.

The simple explanation for the Disney University's success can be attributed to the levels of support and clarity of purpose found in the Four Circumstances, organizational values promoted by Walt Disney and Van France. Both have played a vital role in creating an organizational culture that has sustained "The Happiest Place on Earth" at Disney theme parks for over 57 years.

The Four Circumstances all aim to add value by providing training and guidance to employees.

Circumstance 1: Innovation

Leaders must be *innovative* and comfortable with risk.

Circumstance 2: Organizational Support

Leaders must provide overt, enthusiastic, and sustained *support*; be cheerleaders of employee development!

No one is too big to participate in training at Disney.

Circumstance 3: Education

Employee *education* and development must be woven into organizational culture.

Circumstance 4: Entertain

Employee development ... ranging from the front lines to the executive suite ... must be *entertaining*, engaging, and memorable ... not boring and forgettable.

Disney's Four Circumstances provide a great example of an emphasis on adding value to employees and clients by focusing on distinct areas that are stand-alone added-value principles. The fact that Disney created a Disney University is a huge added-value concept and impacts the culture positively by providing high-level resources and education to the employees. The key advantage that Disney leadership has had over many years is the commitment to creativity, humor, and development with employees and with clients. Today many organizations are recognizing the importance of consistently engaging in these areas for a change and transformation friendly workplace.

WHY YOU?

You are already successful; you would not have picked up a book with this title if you didn't already have a propensity for being a change leader who creates outstanding results. You also likely are driven by a desire for mastery, a desire to be even better, to inspire others at higher levels, to step up your game to the next level. Let's take a look at the WOW approach as a self-assessment tool for you as a change leader.

The WOW approach is a revolutionized SWOT analysis. Although the SWOT is a strategic planning tool that stands for strengths, weaknesses, opportunities, and threats, it is not a tool that focuses on evolutionary change. I have facilitated many strategic retreats using the SWOT, and it has been a useful tool to get everything out on the table and to build a future focus based on the findings and content revealed in the SWOT. However, there is an opportunity to shift the focus of strategic planning to areas in which there is more energy or move-forward focus, which is what the WOW is about. WOW stands for what's working, opportunities, and what's next?

The concept of WOW comes from the development of evolutionary corporate programs based on Epstein Technologies. Epstein Technologies Corporate Content was created from the work of Dr. Donald Epstein who for over 30 years has produced groundbreaking tools for change in the health and wellness arena.

Dr. Epstein is the founder of the Epstein Institute and is a globally renowned thought leader on evolutionary wellness models. He is the creator of reorganizational living models that have application to business, life, and well-being (www .epsteintechnologies.com).

The Epstein Technologies models have been validated by years of research, with their scientific application validated by universities such as University of Southern California, University of California Irvine, University of Wyoming-Laramie, Arizona State University, Massachusetts Institute of Technology, and John F. Kennedy University. Thousands of individuals worldwide have experienced the concepts in a health-delivered format.

In 2014 individuals and businesses began to request organizational application of the Epstein Technologies concepts and models to help improve business and specific business applications such as managing change, improving leadership, growing sales skills, and more.

I work with Dr. Epstein to develop his concepts for corporate application and to bring them to the business arena. Clients such as Sony, Abvie, Asset Management, and more have already benefitted from the groundbreaking programs that have been created for corporate training and education.

I share more information on the Epstein Technologies tools for change later in the book; for now let's look now at the WOW assessment for you as a leader.

WOW Change-Leadership Assessment

1. How would you rate yourself on a scale of 1–10, with 10 being high, on knowing what's working right now for you as a change leader and for your team right now? Why?
2. How would your team members and colleagues rate you on a scale of 1–10, with 10 being high, about your ability to lead change? Why?

3. On a scale of 1–10, with 10 being high, how would you rate yourself as someone who is always seeking opportunities for development/growth? Why?

4. On a scale of 1–10, with 10 being high, how would others on your team, your boss, your colleagues rate you as someone who is always seeking development and growth? Why?

5. On a scale of 1–10, with 10 being high, how would you rate yourself about how you consistently add value to your team, your company, and your clients as a change leader? Why?

6. On a scale of 1–10, with 10 being high, how would you rate yourself on what you do to inspire others and drive transformation in your workplace? Why?

7. On a scale of 1–10, with 10 being high, how would your team and boss rate you about your ability to inspire others and drive transformation in your workplace? Why?

8. On a scale of 1–10, with 10 being high, how would you rate yourself on having a compelling vision for your company, for your team, and for yourself as driver of transformation? Why?

9. What are the opportunities right now for you and for your team, your colleagues and your company?

10. What's next for you and your team and the company? How will you lead the change necessary to achieve what's next?

If your self-assessment ratings were seven and higher, you are well on your way to change leadership mastery. If you rated yourself five or lower on most questions, there is good news: you have the opportunity to learn and grow toward greater success.

The value of self-assessing is to set a new baseline for where we are and to set goals from that baseline.

Notice that rating yourself using the WOW model on a scale of 1–10, as well as answering these questions, focus on what you want to create. Those issues are important from a change leadership standpoint because they provide you with valuable insights into where you are already creating positive change and areas in which you can improve.

In completing the WOW change leadership assessment, you now have a greater sense of the value you bring as a change leader and why your company and the world need you! You will also be more acutely aware of areas where you can step up and become even more masterful at the art of change leadership. For an online version of the WOW assessment template go to www.cherylcran.com/wowassessment.

WHY NOT YOU?

When you think about people who have made big impacts on the world, the initiators, these people have had a bigger vision for the possible future *and* often they have overcome massive challenges in order to create success.

Think of people like Mark Zuckerberg of Facebook, who had an aspiration to build a connection infrastructure for the planet. It was an exceedingly ambitious aspiration, but not too zany given its enormous success. Facebook plays a larger role in human interactions worldwide than any other company. It continues to be a global social phenomenon—a place where you can find and reach out to anyone. More than 900 million people routinely spend time there. Facebook continues to be a movement—that's the vision that Zuckerberg himself has had since he began in 2007. It's easy to see Zuckerberg as a change leader and to think of him more as a social evolutionary than a businessperson.

Zuckerberg has *convinced the world to change* by creating an added value application for people's lives through a social media platform. His vision was and is to fulfill the vision he and his friends have had since he was 19—that the world could be transformed by connection, open sharing of information, thoughts, and ideas.

How do you think Zuckerberg would rate on the preceding WOW self-assessment? Why?

You may not be a Zuckerberg or even aspire to be like him yet you impact and inspire your circle of influence. What is the difference between a Zuckerberg or you or me? We all have a contribution to make and the contributions that each of us makes creates a ripple effect on those around us. The biggest opportunity for you as a change leader is to step up to the next level of contribution and to inspire others to make the changes needed to make progress.

In order to inspire and lead others, we must identify our own fears or doubts and then focus on the bigger contribution and the bigger purpose of why you are here, right now and in this place. It *has* to be you to lead the change necessary to transform your life, your work, and the world. A good friend of mine and colleague, Dr. John Izzo, is the author of the book, *Stepping Up—How Taking Responsibility Changes Everything*, and in it he talks about the courage and the commitment it takes to step up. In the book he describes the difference between being a victim and an influencer. He conducted an online survey entitled, "Why Don't You Step Up?"

The online survey was of 325 people, mostly professionals, who responded from across the United States and Canada and the results were as follows:

46 percent of the respondents had the belief that they can't change things and that they are only one person.

20 percent of the respondents said that it's other people's responsibility.

18 percent of the respondents said they are caught up in the daily grind.

16 percent of the respondents said they feared looking bad if nothing changes.

The results of this survey are interesting to me; almost half of those who responded believe that they can't change things and that they are only one person. Do you think Zuckerberg ever had that thought? Maybe, but he sure didn't waste time there if he did! If not you, who?

The belief that you are only one person is a cop-out, an excuse to accept the status quo; to do nothing; and to not have to claim responsibility for taking a stand, for taking action, and for making a difference. Apathy is the enemy of change!

You as a change leader already know this and there must be consistent vigilance on focusing on the compelling future, the compelling opportunities, and the change that needs to be created in the workplaces all around the world. Change becomes easier when it is less about us and feeling small and more about how the change will benefit more and more people. Many change leaders may not become famous and yet their impact has a lasting legacy. I am thinking of people who saw a need, those who saw that something *had* to change and took action to make it so.

Rosa Parks, Martin Luther King Jr., Abraham Lincoln, Maya Angelou—all made change that stemmed from the desire to set a new standard, to say no to the status quo, and to create a better future for more people.

The following story is about young change leaders who saw a need and made change—a great example of not accepting the status quo. A group of three Ukrainian students had a vision to make the world an easier place to navigate for the hearing impaired.

Their compelling vision was to give a voice to the voiceless. This team of Ukrainian students had the vision to improve and simplify the lives of the hearing impaired and to create a glove that would translate sign language into vocalized speech via a smartphone.

The inspiration for the gloves came from observing fellow college students who were hearing impaired and who were having a difficult time communicating and interacting with other students. The result of the communication challenges was that the hearing impaired students would often be excluded from activities.

The Ukrainian team motto is "we're giving a voice to movements," and they have launched Enable Talk (enabletalk.com), a website that openly shares their ambitious vision, design documentation, and business plan for how to bring the device to market. Furthermore, the team is looking into the possibility of enabling the same technology to allow cell phone conversations using the system.

That could mean a new way for about 70 million people with hearing and speech impairments to verbally communicate and connect to people around them. The power to be a change leader grows exponentially when the vision and the goals are way bigger and beyond the self as this young team of Ukrainian students demonstrates.

So again I ask, why not *you*?

A few more questions for you to think about as a change leader:

- How can you shift your current vision for the future and for the changes you want to lead to an even bigger and more compelling vision?
- What would your personal mission statement be for your new compelling vision?
- How many people do you want to help as a result of your change leadership? Why?

These questions help to raise the commitment and to set a new standard for the impact that you will make on others. Your company, your family, and your life deserve to have new standards and new levels of contribution that bring more energy and life into what you do.

The other survey result, in which 20 percent of the respondents said that making change was other people's responsibility, is an unfortunate one. The attitude that "it's not my responsibility" really gets my goat. Why? Because saying that someone else has to change first is a very narrow perspective and it is not the belief that will drive transformation. In a company of change leaders, *all* are required to commit to being a part of the change. It's a low energy, self-focused attitude that separates—not connects—teams of people. Frankly, organizations cannot move forward and create the change required with this attitude. The opportunity to shift this belief from a disempowering one to a fully empowered one is vast. How?

We need to inspire and create a story for those who have this belief, a compelling story where he or she or you are the hero. A belief in the reality that everyone is a leader. The future workplace is about shared leadership; it's not about someone else being the one to take initiative. It's about everyone being a leader and leading change collectively. Tony Hsieh, the CEO of Zappos, created a clever way of ensuring that all members of the employee base within his company were agents of change. He introduced the holocracy model into the company in 2014. Holocracy is a shared leadership model that was created a number of years ago with a few companies adopting its methodologies. It is a self-organizing philosophy where teams share leadership and everyone is accountable for team results. There is a great video on YouTube that explains it more fully. The link is https://www.youtube.com/watch?v=-DYigfNJQlg. There is also a follow-up video about how it's going here: https://www.youtube.com/watch?v=EG02dmwWN8w.

When anyone thinks that leading change is not his or her responsibility, it means that they have either had previous experiences in which he or she made the effort to make a change and was admonished or was not given any positive feedback. The other scenario is a workplace culture that is not change responsive and the employees have learned to not rock the boat for fear of being fired or getting a bad performance review. Alternatively, an individual may have an inner compass that guides them to look out for number one (self) while not seeing the value of stepping up to lead change for self and others because of no apparent reward or reason. The irony with being the person to lead change is the immense value that comes from creating more energy, inspiration, and value for self *and* for others.

In other words, you need to see it as yours and others' absolute imperative that leading change is *everyone's* responsibility in today's fast paced and changing world.

Imagine what would have happened if Candace Lynn Lightner had not seen it as her responsibility to put an end to drunk driving. Candy Lightner started Mothers Against Drunk Driving on May 7, 1980, four days after the tragedy of her daughter Cari being hit by a drunk driver and a day after Cari's funeral. She had discovered that the offender, who had been caught, would probably not receive any time in jail for his crime. She promised herself on the day of Cari's death that she would fight to make this needless homicide count for something positive in the years ahead.

She saw the need to lead a much-needed change not just as a result of her and her family's loss but also for the betterment of all parents for years to come. Candace had a vision to make the world a better place by having fewer drunk drivers on the road.

The goal of her organization was to raise public awareness of the serious nature of drunk driving and to promote tough legislation against the crime.

Prior to Candy Lightner's crusade, drunk driving was not taken seriously. Some comedians actually made a career of impersonating drunken people on stage. Intoxication was often used as an excuse for otherwise unacceptable behavior and the excuse of "I didn't know what I was doing—I was drunk."

Lightner's approach was to put human faces on the victims of drunk drivers. Statistics weren't simply a collection of numbers; instead, each number represented an individual who was *needlessly* killed. She helped people realize that deaths caused by drunk driving were not an acceptable inevitability.

Candace could have chosen to be bitter and angry for the rest of her life about the unfairness of the situation. Instead, she chose to be the leader of change—to not leave it to someone else but to make it her legacy to save thousands of lives through greater awareness about nonproductive and harmful behavior such as drunk driving. What if Candace had not stepped up? She transformed her personal grief and loss into a crusade for ensuring that other mothers would not have to experience the same loss—she became an agent for change and transformation.

The other survey results from the "Why Don't You Step Up" survey indicated that 18 percent said they were too busy with the daily grind to be a leader of change. Time is a reality that all contend with; with the fast paced world everyone expects real-time answers and responses. Technology has sped up the way we work and live, and this has caused many people to feel the trap of not enough time. If we look at time through the lens of change leadership as a reason to not step up, is time a valid reason? Do we justify putting off valuable actions because of time? We all have the same 24 hours in a day, and the most pro-ductive use of time is engaging in activities that move goals and visions forward. Taking the time to step up and to lead change, making the time to create better systems and solutions that ulti-mately would save more time requires the desire to invest the time now in order to reap the rewards later of stepping up. For example, many leaders will often tell me that they do not have the time to coach or to do an employee performance review. Really what they are saying is that they don't value investing time in these activities. If leaders do not value the investment of time for people development, then they need to rethink their roles as leaders! Time invested is time that is rewarded. This holds true for anything of value that anyone wants to create. Want to have happy, well-adjusted children? Invest quality time in playing with, being with, guiding, and engaging with your children. Want to have a healthy and fit body? Invest the time into the behaviors such as eating well and moving the body to gain the rewards. Want to have a work team that is autonomous, solution oriented, and contains leaders of change? Invest the time in coaching, training, and valuing your employees.

You get the point. Saying that you don't have time simply shows where you place value. If you don't take the time to step up to lead change, you do not value the power of your contribution to make a positive change for the better. Simple.

The last response to the "Why Don't You Step Up" survey was 16 percent who were afraid of looking bad if nothing changed as a result of him or her leading the change. This fear is one in which an individual has established a pattern believing that taking risks is dangerous and failure is fatal. Somehow, he or she has been conditioned to be risk averse when it comes to stepping up or leading change. This response tells me that the individuals who answered in this way have wired the brain to believe that doing nothing is better than doing something. The problem with this belief is that an individual will continue to be passive and will constantly struggle with the push and pull of not getting the respect that he or she desires and not taking action for fear of getting it wrong. Nothing great has happened without very brave and courageous people risking failure. In fact, many successful people have admitted that it has been their perceived failures that have led them to their greatness.

People like Thomas Edison who was famously quoted as saying, "I have not failed. I just found 10,000 ways that won't work." Or this quote from Michael Jordan, "I can accept failure; everyone fails at something. But I can't accept not trying." And, finally, how about Bill Gates: "It's fine to celebrate successes but far more important to heed the lessons of failure."

WHY DO WE NEED YOU?

Regardless of where you are on the change leader range (you are beginning to take change leader steps or you are ready to take the next big momentous step as a change leader), we need people like you to say: "I am here right now and right here and I will give all of my gifts of change leadership to make an even bigger impact on my workplace, my life, and the world."

WHY NOW?

Earlier, I mentioned a colleague, Dr. Epstein. One of his quotes speaks to why we must have change leaders now: "There is too much information in the world right now and not enough wisdom to organize it."

We need change leaders who can increase and share wisdom for others to navigate the fast pace of change, the speed of technological innovation, and the increasing demands from clients and employees.

A real change leader unlocks not only his or her full potential but also the potential of everyone that he or she connects with. He or she harnesses the evolutionary calling to be a change agent to create the greater good that businesses can create, to be a model of truth, to lead others to be in harmony, to demonstrate justice, and to promote equality. The art of change leadership is the call to find solutions for the problems that plague humanity right now in a fast paced world.

So why now? The basic reality: what the world needs *now* is *more* change leaders focused on a drive for transformation. We need more change leaders at every level in every kind of organization: businesses, government, schools, professional associations, and unions.

With change, crisis, and complexity coming at us faster and faster from all directions, we cannot depend on just a few leaders to lead change.

John Kotter, author of *Leading Change*, defines leadership as "creating a vision of the future and strategies for producing the changes needed to achieve that vision; aligning people around the vision; and motivating them to overcome barriers and produce the changes needed to achieve the vision."

How many change leaders do we need (including you)?

We need as many change leaders as it takes to make a major impact on a planet of 7 billion people.

The time is now for today's organizations to unlock the change leadership potential within the company so that those who demonstrate desire and willingness to lead change get the opportunity. From the CEO and the executive team to middle managers to supervisors, the time is now to make a bigger commitment to be leaders of change.

Why now?

We cannot wait to build cultures in which the vision for the future is clearly understood throughout the organization. We cannot procrastinate building a culture in which people are invited to step forward to help advance the vision and mission in micro and macro ways. We must commit now to lead a change culture in which failures are seen as innovation intersections and an opportunity for growth and learning. We must have the courage *now* to create cultures in which transparency is the new norm and everyone dares to be open. There is no time to waste to create a culture that celebrates wins both large and small. As change leaders, the calling is for us to lead a change leadership culture in which one rarely hears the phrases, "That's not your job," or "That's not my job." Rather, the phrases heard throughout the company are, "Let's find out how to do this" and "Let's brainstorm creative solutions."

YOUR 30-, 60-, AND 90-DAY PERSONAL PLAN AS A CHANGE LEADER

I will share the components of the change process for leading others through change and for organizational change later in the book, but here I want to ensure that you make a further commitment to enhancing your personal change leadership skills.

30-Day Plan

For the next 30 days, make a commitment to take the following actions:

1. Make time to do the WOW assessment in this chapter.
2. Based on your answers to the WOW assessment, set goals for the areas that you identify as opportunities for you to develop.
3. Ask three people who work with you to assess your personal change leadership approach. Ask them to be honest and to share areas of opportunity for you to improve.
4. Do one thing differently in your weekly personal routine to mix things up: maybe change where you get your coffee or tea or change your route to work or your workout routine.
5. Create an updated and inspiring vision and personal mission statement. You can use the online tool provided by Franklin Covey to help you with this. Go to www.cherylcran.com/actionplans for more information and then make it your screen saver or set an alarm to remind you of it daily.

60-Day Plan

1. Focus on personal creativity and innovation—research ways to be more creative. Read the ebook version of *How to Think Like Leonardo Di Vinci* and do a few of the exercises in the book.

2. During your commute or while you are working out, listen to audio books of autobiographies of inspirational change leaders. Steve Jobs's biography by Walter Isaacson is a well-written and inspiring book on the creative genius of Jobs.

3. Follow creative people on Twitter, Pinterest, and Instagram and pay attention to how they creatively communicate with their followers. Use this as inspiration on how you can do the same.

90-Day Plan

1. With every problem or fire that has to be put out, practice going to a creative question as your primary response—practice asking yourself, "What is a solution that will not only solve the problem but do so in a way that is creative?"

2. Practice thinking in a way that puts two things together to create new uses. For example, an exercise I often do with audiences to promote creative thinking is to have them, in small groups, list 10 things that a cat and refrigerator or a dog and a stove have in common; the key is thinking beyond the status quo.

3. Do the WOW self-assessment again to see how you have improved and to set goals for the next 90-day cycle.

Make sure you celebrate and recognize the progress you are making as a change leader. Notice how leading change and stepping up increases your energy and your focus. Come back and redo the 30-, 60-, and 90-day actions again.

Hack the Status Quo: Change Manager or Change Leader?

We make a living by what we get, but we make a life by what we give.

—Winston Churchill

There are numerous definitions of change management; there are broad and varied interpretations of the two words. The *BNET Business Dictionary* version is quite good: "The coordination of a structured period of transition from situation A to situation B in order to achieve lasting change within an organization."

Wikipedia's version is: "Change management is a structured approach to transitioning individuals, teams, and organizations from a current state to a desired future state. The current definition of Change Management includes both organizational change management processes and individual change management models, which together are used to manage the people side of change."

Although change management has been a focus for organizations for over 20 years, it seems there is still a challenge to effect lasting change for most companies and the people within the companies. Why?

Because as much as we can bring a systematic process to create change, the one variable that requires the most focus and the most time is helping individuals become more change adept. Change creates different responses from different people for a variety of reasons. Simply applying a change management process that involves tactical and project management skills will not produce long-lasting change in a culture. The people within the organization need to claim the new version of themselves and how they see themselves fitting within the new version of the future company. This is why change management has not produced the results that many businesses seek when setting out to turn the company in a new direction.

The solution in my opinion is to shift the language around change and create a new lexicon that guides people to desire growth and newness and expanded impact on the world.

What we need are change leaders, leaders of transformation with the skills to inspire, inform, guide, coach, and propel people forward to the future promise of a new vision built upon past successes.

WHAT'S THE DIFFERENCE BETWEEN A CHANGE MANAGER OR A CHANGE LEADER?

The differences between a change manager and a change leader are distinct. See Table 3.1.

As you can see from Table 3.1, the ideal change leader would be a hybrid of both the change manager and change leader. The skill set needed for today and the future workplace requires an integration of the skills in the chart below and most importantly a focus on people and heart. You can get your free copy of this chart at www.cherylcran.com/changeleaderchart.

Table 3.1   The Differences between Change Managers and Change
Leaders

	Change Manager	Change Leader
Actions	Creates a plan, directs projects and people to achieve a goal	Sets the compelling vision; tells a story that includes the hero's journey for each person involved
Personality Distinctions	Rational, problem solver, private, focused on goals, uses structures and processes, analytical and logical.	Charismatic, warm, open, inspirational, takes risks, relational, has creative ideas; focused on big picture
Primary Focus	Managing work and tasks	Leading and coaching people
Preferred Focus	Tasks	People
Approach with Employees	Involved	Facilitative
Traits	Authoritative, autocratic, dictatorial, consultative, and democratic	Transformational, consultative, and participative
Power Through	Position and authority	Inspiration and influence
Appeals to	Head	Heart
Strengths	Structure, direction, process, plan, goals, steps to be taken, and measuring success	Influencer, appeals to emotion of people, big picture, takes risks, sets compelling vision

When we look at the evolution of the workplace over the past 20 years, the workplace culture itself in most companies was structured to have mostly workplace managers not leaders. The workplace and the impacts shaping the workplace have changed dramatically from the 1980s when authority was where the power was, when employees respected the boss purely due to title and age. There were distinct hierarchies in the workplace and there were processes and protocols that everyone followed.

Fast forward to the late 1990s and the 2000s and there were many companies that went through downsizing, major restructures, and going out of business. The changes thrust upon organizations due to economic and technological innovation forced many leaders and their teams to adhere to an autocratic and dictatorial approach with a lets-get-things-done attitude. I call it the "push" rather than the "pull" approach to change leadership, when a leader uses force versus power. When facilitating groups on change, I will often ask the group to put their hands up palm to palm to the people that they are seated beside and then I instruct them that when I say "go" someone needs to push.

Inevitably everyone pushes. Why?

The obvious answer is because I told them to, but did I really? I said that *someone* has to push, but always everyone pushes. The answer is a psychological one because for every action there is an equal and opposite reaction. This is a powerful concept as it relates to being a change leader. A change manager will typically and consistently push his or her ideas, thoughts, expectations, and criticisms onto the people they lead. The result is that people respond by pushing back. It's human nature. Therefore, one of the many benefits of learning to be a change leader is the art of creating movement by flexing and adapting to others in order to create forward momentum. I demonstrate this by asking the group to once again put up their hands palm to palm and this time someone pushes and someone gives. Often there is a pause and confusion before someone tentatively pushes and the other relaxes and gives. This second time around the outcome is one that is more in alignment with a change-leader's outcome because, if a change leader is willing to flex and shift to the other person, there is movement; there is a pull toward rather than a reaction against or resistant response. There are a few outcomes such as the person pushing finds himself or herself easing up on the pushing when the other person gives. The second outcome is the person who gives actually creates movement and momentum and holds a lot of power with that ability. The third outcome in that exercise is that neither person pushes, which is an ideal neutral resting ground, because it allows space to openly discuss alternatives before a decision is made or an action is taken. As you can see from this exercise, in the first part, when everyone pushes, there is an obvious link between the change manager approach, which is to push ideas, thoughts, demands, power, and more, which will always create a pushback or change-resistant response from others.

In the second part, when someone pushes and someone gives is what a change leader uses as a skill and an ability to create movement and to bring people along with the change willingly rather than push back.

LANGUAGE OF A CHANGE LEADER

Recently I blogged about the need for a new language for the new workplace and how one of the ways to create more flexibility and movement as change leaders is with the language that we choose.

I am sharing the blog post here as an example of how Generation Ys specifically respond to positive language rather than "push-back" language.

> **Blog Post March 11, 2015**
> The evolution of leadership from autocratic to inclusive is a journey that many leaders are still looking to master. Making the change from a mind-set of authority and power toward a mind-set of sharing successes and equalization of power is a big one.
>
> One of the key ingredients of leading change is the ability to lead with the new leadership language that is required

to inspire and engage today's workforce and to set the tone for the future workplace.

You have heard the phrase "You can get more flies with honey than vinegar" and it has never been more needed than in today's workplace. Research has shown that Gen Ys (those in their 20s to early 30s) do not respond to the criticism that many Traditionalists and Zoomers (baby boomers who refuse to age) have had to endure. However Gen Ys do respond to coaching, feedback, and skill development, aka "honey."

If you say to a Gen Y, "It took me 30 years to get here, kid, and unless you work as hard as I did you are never going to make it"—that is not going to inspire and engage anyone let alone a Gen Y.

Instead if you say to a Gen Y, "My goal for you is to far surpass me in your career and I want to help you get there. It's going to take focus and effort on your part but I will give you all the tools to succeed in less time than it took me," you will not only have an inspired and engaged Gen Y; you will have created longer loyalty.

The difference in energy in each of those statements is simply that the first statement is about power, authority, and bringing the Gen Y down a notch. The second statement, when said sincerely, requires a leader who has gotten over the ego of himself or herself and, instead, focuses on creating shared value for both employees and clients.

The future workplace requires everyone to engage in language that is inclusive, valuing of the people's personality, gender, generation, and work style, and focused on creative solutions.

The new language comes from rewiring the brain to think in ways that create shared value, that bring energy and enthusiasm to others, and that focus on success for all.

The language example used in the preceding blog post about criticism versus inspiring is well articulated in a clip that I often use from the movie, *In Good Company*, in which the

Gen Y leader uses creativity and inspiration to get the entire company on board with his ideas and direction. Frankly it is this type of language and enthusiasm that *everyone* wants, not just a single generation. The difference is that many who are in their mid 50s to late 60s (Zoomers) were raised by highly critical parents, which led to being highly self-critical, which then led to the natural tendency to criticize others including spouse, children, and employees. Zoomer parents encouraged the Gen Xs and Gen Ys and raised Gen Xs and Ys to find work that they loved and to negotiate with their teachers and to stand up for their rights. The result is two generations who do not respond to criticism and who *do* respond to inspirational coaching, guidance and the providing of resources. The truth is that Zoomers and their Traditionalist parents didn't know any better. What is that phrase—"know better and do better?" We now know better about the power of language and positive feedback and so the current workplace is demanding that we change to consistently do better.

Table 3.2 shows language differences between a change manager and a change leader.

Obtain your free at-a-glance copy of this chart at www.cheryl cran.com/languagechart.

From Table 3.2, you can see the difference in approaches and language with the situations used. The key distinction is that a change manager focuses mostly on self and does not factor in the value of the other individual. A change leader values *all* people and shows that value by speaking to them as a valued member of the team with respect and by providing tools for the team member to succeed.

One more distinction between a change manager and a change leader I would like to make is the Epstein Technologies concepts that I spoke about earlier. This concept concerns restore and reorganize.

Table 3.2   Language Differences between a Change Manager and a
Change Leader

Situations	Change Manager	Change Leader
Hiring	You will have to work extremely hard to make it here; it takes years to achieve any amount of success.	We are a culture of results; we focus on working together as a team where everyone is responsible to create stellar results. The people who work as team members get ahead quickly here.
Performance feedback	You need to be better at customer service; our customer survey showed that you did not know the solutions for the customer. You need to improve this or your job is at stake.	Customer service is a vital component to your overall performance. We would like to support you by providing customer service training. I will meet with you every two weeks to review what you have learned.
Promotion	You have only been here three months and you want a promotion! Do you know how long it took me to get to where I am? When I was your age I did whatever I was told in order to get ahead.	Our company recognizes high performers. In the three months that you have been here I have observed your skills at leveraging technology *and* I would like to see you focus on linking your technology skills to the business, as well as see you learn to communicate even more effectively with your clients. Let's review your progress in the next three-month cycle.
Learning a new technology	I know you have been here for over 20 years and technology is not your thing, but if you don't learn it you will have problems. Get with the times!	Your experience and contributions have been many over the years. It would really benefit you and your team to learn how to leverage the new technology in order to speed up processes for our clients. Let me pair you up with a team member who can show you hands on how to maximize the technology. Trust me—once you learn it you will wonder why you didn't always use it as a useful tool.

Dr. Epstein found that in human behavior and also in organizations there is a tendency for many people or the culture of an organization to be focused on how to get things to the way they were before, which is restore. Restore would be the push-back example, in which a person may have the attitude that they don't want anything to change, they just want to remain in the comfort of certainty and to know that things will remain a constant. There is a balance between certainty and uncertainty that can be used to create a dynamic life, a dynamic leader, and a dynamic workplace culture. A change manager is geared more toward a restore approach because as a manager of change he or she is trying to mitigate or control change. This restore quote by Dr. Epstein sums it up nicely:

> When people choose a restorative change they often lower their standards and actually end up living with less than they had before even though their goal is "getting back to how it used to be," to a previous known point of safety.

The concept of reorganization is that greater success is created by focusing on ways to get to a higher level of success than before. A change leader is constantly focused on reorganizing. The word *reorganization* often gets a bad rap in the corporate world because so many people have been through restructures and downsizing. The word *reorganization* from Dr. Epstein's work is used as a way of looking at personal and business change in a way that promotes growth and opportunity for everyone. The key aspects of being a change leader focused on reorganization are:

- Goes beyond the status quo to create a new level or version.
- Sees disruption as an invitation to improvement.
- Has the courage to be focused on reorganization.

The following quote on reorganization by Donny Epstein succinctly clarifies it as a tool in the toolbox for change leaders.

> Reorganize is about taking any current pain (life or business) and using it as an opportunity to create more of what we truly desire. When a painful event or life circumstance occurs we focus on what new and amazing opportunity it is presenting that we never would have seen or chosen before.
>
>   —Dr. Donald Epstein

The global economic challenges that occurred in 2008 were a pain that many people had to go through. If we look at the 2008 disruption through the lens of restore versus reorganization we could easily identify those people who wanted things to go back to the way they were and those who saw the need to reorganize to a new economic reality.

The change leaders needed today are those who do not hesitate to make the changes needed based on what is happening in the marketplace or in their lives; they immediately seek to organize to a higher level. A change leader does not strive to hold on to the past or the good-old days; rather, he or she enthusiastically sees disruption as an opportunity to step up to a new level of success.

Change management includes processes and keeping it under control. Change leadership puts a massive energy turbine on the change to make things faster, better, and stronger. Change management works well with smaller changes, whereas change leadership is scaleable for large changes.

Change management tries to minimize disruptions and focuses on things such as keeping you from going over budget. Typically, there are change-management groups and task forces that are given the goal of "push this forward," but with control.

Change leadership is urgent, it includes large amounts of people who want to see things happen, and it empowers lots of people. Change leadership has less control and more space for creativity guided with a highly skilled leadership team that moves change forward while keeping an eye on risk but not focusing on risk. Change leadership is linked to bigger leaps and taking advantage of openings and opportunities in a faster and responsive way. We need leaders to get better at change leadership because it requires people who have the courage to make change for the good of all.

When you think of a company like Kodak, do you think change management or change leadership?

In 1996, Kodak was ranked the world's fourth most-valuable brand behind Disney, Coca-Cola, and McDonald's. Then the digital revolution happened. Did you know that Kodak had had the digital camera and digital technology since the early 1970s? However, they did not take a change-leadership approach. They did not take the opportunity of using market leaders in all things digital. They clung to the film aspect of the business. An article in *The Economist* states that Kodak had become a complacent monopolist. In other words Kodak did not have a balance of change leaders and change managers and the rest, as they say, is history.

For companies not having change leaders, their risk today is whether the company still be in business a few years from now.

The fast pace of change that includes newer and evolving technologies requires innovative and prescient change leaders in order to thrive.

THE CHANGE LEADER'S APPROACH TO DRIVE TRANSFORMATION

The change leader's approach to drive transformation includes the integration of a change leader's attributes and change-manager processes. The contrast between a change manager and a change leader is necessary so that there is a clear distinction between the two approaches. The point is not to create polarity or to have a reason to now point fingers at your co-workers and call him or her out for being a change manager versus a change leader. The opportunity is to take the good and the necessary skills of the change manager approach and leverage with the change-leader approach.

From the tables shown earlier in this chapter, it is clear that a pure change-manager approach is authoritative, dictatorial, and about minimizing risk. The change leader approach on its own is about inspiration, direction, and emotional intelligence. Together the combination of skills and approaches are the magic formula for dynamic change leadership.

The skill set, then, of an integrated change leader includes the following:

- Sets a compelling vision while honoring past successes.
- Provides a project timeline while creating celebration milestones.
- Connects personally with individuals to "onboard" them to the changes and provides the framework for how the changes will happen.
- Cheerleads and champions change agents while continually providing data and progress results to the change averse.
- Consistently inspires, encourages, and rewards efforts while providing structures for ongoing communication

in a variety of formats including face to face, text, e-mail, video conferencing, and more.

- Courageously leads the changes without falter while being open and honest about his or her own fears and challenges along the change journey.
- Constantly looks to provide added value to the team members by customizing feedback, providing resources and support.
- Keeps an eye on risk while driving changes forward with momentum.
- Welcomes disruptions and leverages them into new creative solution opportunities for self and for the teams.
- Involves all stakeholders and shares leadership with operations, finance, sales, marketing, customer service, and human resources.
- Focuses on holding multiple perspectives that include the perspective of self, perspective of individuals, perspectives of executive, perspectives of clients and suppliers.
- Sees putting out fires as an integral component to being a change leader and coaches the problem-solving skills for others to creatively find solutions for repetitive challenges.
- Willingly shares power with others with a depth of confidence and without having the need to protect ego or CYA.
- Integrates the logics of the head/mind with the emotional intelligence of the heart knowing that change leadership is about emotionally engaging people into connecting to the change.
- Sees the role of a change leader as a facilitator of intelligence and not as the keeper of all knowledge and power.

For your at-a-glance copy of this list to share with your teams go to www.cherylcran.com/changeleaderskillset.

As you can see from this list, being a change leader could be viewed as difficult and a lot of work! A master change leader requires the commitment, the desire, and the calling to the hero's journey to see him or her as part of the change they want to see in the world.

HOW DO YOU INTEGRATE BEING A CHANGE MANAGER WITH BEING A CHANGE LEADER?

The perennial question is how does one become a master change leader who is integrated with the change manager and change leadership?

There are a variety of ways to become more masterful, and some of these ideas may be familiar to you and some of the other ideas I share with you may be too way out there for you. I ask you to remain open and to choose what feels like a good resource or direction for you and who you are.

I will be sharing more of the "out-there" tools in Chapter 4. Well, they may not seem so "out there" to you being the change leader that you are!

First you must understand whether you are more of a change manager or more of a change leader. Take the quick assessment that follows next, and, once you have self-scored, take a look at actions you can take to become more integrated and more masterful.

Change Manager/Change Leader Assessment

1. When faced with a personal change (divorce/job change/ health) do you:
   a. Resist it at first and then warm up to the idea.
   b. Find fault with the change without having all of the facts.

    c. Eagerly anticipate the growth and opportunity of the change.

    d. Worry and get anxious over the impact of the change.

2. In your opinion the best way to deal with change is:

    a. Deal with the facts and remain logical.

    b. Analyze the impact, assess the risk impact, and have data that supports the change.

    c. Focus on the big picture, strategize the easiest and fastest way to get to the next level.

    d. Wait and see how the change affects others before forming an opinion.

3. You have a major change that the entire company needs to buy into. Would you:

    a. Lay out the plan, the process, and who needs to do what?

    b. Protect the company and mitigate the risks?

    c. Organize a company-wide meeting and present the disruption that is forcing the need for transformation, ask for everyone's ideas, and then share immediate next steps?

    d. Share it with the senior leadership and hope that the rest of the company doesn't get wind of the upcoming change?

4. Your company changes the way it rewards its employees by focusing on performance versus tenure. How would you feel about this change?

    a. You would be angry—don't they know how long you have worked there?

    b. You would review the new reward system and calculate the impact on yourself and other long-time colleagues in order to dispute the change.

c. You would celebrate the change, because you are confident in your performance results regardless of your tenure.

d. You would be apathetic—here we go again—the company is changing the way it deals with employees… again!

5. Your company has many employees who are Generation X and Y and collectively they want human resources to establish a policy that allows all workers to work from home for three days a week. You would:

a. Be worried that people won't work as hard if they are working from home three days a week.

b. You would research the cost and the impact of this change on the company from a financial and customer service standpoint and make a case for why it won't work.

c. You would be happy to participate in working from home three days a week because it allows you to be more flexible with your time.

d. You would miss the camaraderie of having the majority of workers in the office all at once. You would be sad about this because you prefer to work in an office environment, not from home.

If you answered mostly a's and b's on this questionnaire, you lean more toward a change-manager approach. If you answered mostly c's you have mostly a change-leadership approach and if you answered mostly d's you are not keen on change overall and unconsciously prefer to keep things the way they are.

The great part of having assessment opportunities is to reestablish your awareness of where you are and use the new level of awareness to set goals for growth.

For an online version of the Change Manager/Change Leader Assessment that you can use in your company please go to www.cherylcran.com/mgr_leaderassessment.

I have the great fortune of working with many successful leaders and business owners in my line of work. Recently I worked with a client who wanted to shift the direction of the company in a completely new direction. The company is Omnitel, a communications firm that, for the past 20 years or so was a telephone company, and in the past few years recognizes that it is now a technology firm.

This change in identity of the brand has caused the need for the entire company to turn around 360 degrees and restrategize its approach.

I interviewed two of the executives, Josh Hveem and Gary Schotanus, on the changes they knew they needed to make and how they leveraged the change leadership tools to transform the company.

The interview provides fantastic insight into how individuals need to make the mind-set changes before leading the company in the new direction. Change leaders influence change rapidly and effectively when integrated with change management steps.

Interview with Josh and Gary—Omnitel

Cheryl: What are the changes you have been forced to go through because of industry changes?

Josh/Gary: We found that the industry overall was forcing us to make some pretty big organizational changes. In our case we had a senior leadership group who had

(Continued)

longevity and who were great assets; however, when it became evident that the market changes required much faster strategies, we had to reevaluate if we had the right people on board. In our case we made the tough decision to have some team members leave. Sometimes players have to leave when a big change happens—after our change leadership strategy planning session we had with you over a year ago it was evident that a number of people had to go. We saw that key leadership roles were crucial to being competitive and that we had to have the "right people in the right seats" as we drove forward toward transformation.

We implemented company-wide employee surveys to obtain candid feedback before and after the leadership changes. Then we very much focused on building relationships and letting our employees know that we heard them, we were supporting them, and we spent a lot of time on getting everyone on board before and after we made changes.

When we did make the changes, the company transformed almost overnight; nobody really believed that we as the senior leadership team would implement even a quarter of an actual plan because, in the past, we did not have the right leaders in place who followed through.

Cheryl: What did you do to help gain company-wide buy-in from all stakeholders once you had made the changes at the top leadership level?

Gary/Josh: Making the changes at the top senior leadership level created the desired effect of deeper trust because we had taken the employee feedback from the surveys to heart. We then immediately set out to implement the changes of roles and capacities of all employees to better match skill sets with jobs. We spent time on project planning and following our change leadership plan by having preparation meetings one-on-one with all employees, coaching meetings individually to assess their feedback on what needed to change in the company, and then we engaged them with how things were going to change. We communicated the timeline and we kept up ongoing communications throughout each phase of the changes. What we did required tenacity as we made big changes in a company that is very well known in our small rural community. We had to communicate a positive message to the community in addition to our employees. The community responded positively because our focus was on providing superior customer service to them. We took a caring approach to all aspects of the changes with regard to our customers, to those who had to leave, and to our employees who had been promised big changes. We then set out to transform the way forward by setting a standard of performance, a culture of fun and performance.

Cheryl: What are some the mind-set changes that had to happen among the people in order to drive this transformation forward for your company?

Josh/Gary: When we analyzed the results of the employee surveys prior to making the big changes in our senior leadership team, we quickly realized that the current team of leaders wasn't going to make the necessary changes and were not ready to make the mind-set shifts needed to go in the direction we needed to go, which was to shift from a telephone company to a full technology firm. When we met with the previous senior leadership team, we agreed that we needed to have a higher

(Continued)

standard for being held accountable for the direction of company. The senior leaders who were not ready and able to make swift mind-set changes to the new direction literally recognized they were not willing or able to be the change leaders to drive the busines forward self-selected. themselves out of their jobs. Why? Because the employee surveys made it blatantly obvious the type of leadership needed to move forward.

The mind-set needed by all employees from top down was to be focused on progress, accountability, customer value, and working together. We reorganized our senior leadership team so that everyone on the team had change leadership and transformation mind-set approaches.

After the renewed senior leadership team of change leaders committed to the future vision was presented to the employees, there was a great response—for example people who had been pigeonholed in a position and had tremendous capabilities for themselves and the company but were never given the opportunity. Now, with the changes and the freed energy toward innovation, there was renewed energy and focus for the entire company.

Cheryl: Can you give an example of a structure change you made as a result of this focus on transformation?

Gary/Josh: We realized that if we were shifting to a performance-based culture, we would need to change the performance review process to a questionnaire format that included a focus on what the employee wants to do. We said, "Lets burn the org chart." We aligned interests with abilities and we put it to work, and we now have a lot more happy employees. Together we are implementing and working with aligned interests with what we are creating. Instead of senior leadership dictating, we are co-creating the org chart—we are transforming the company together—with the employees input and, together, we have set the vision.

Cheryl: What are some of the changes in mind-set each of you have had to personally make in order to lead Omnitel through its renaissance as a technology company not a telephone company?

Josh/Gary: For each of us, it was not so much a complete change in mind-set as we were not part of the previous culture of longevity and entitlement. We were more on the periphery and separate from the telecom past issues and we were not part of the day-to-day minutiae. We both have always had the mind-set that is identical, which is "no excuses!"

We focus our time and energy on continual coaching and getting employees to buy into the new performance mind-set. Many barriers have been broken and, of course, there is still left over mistrust from the previous embedded mind-set, and transformation is not over. Because of any single win, we have the mind-set that we must be vigilant in communicating the vision for the company and engaging everyone in the focus on the new culture. We have the mind-set that we can all work together—we are all in!

Gary: I came from a technology company and brought the mind-set that we needed to operate as a full-fledged technology company. It was difficult for me when I first came to this company because the previous cultural mind-set was that the company was only a telephone company. This limited perspective of who we were as a company presented much challenge in being competitive with our customers. We are now focused on continual innovation, and we have moved into being more about

(Continued)

adding value to both our employees and customers. We now want only people on our team, including ourselves, to be problem solvers and creative-solution providers. We had to share the new mind-set with every single person who remained in the company, and we are seeing ongoing transformation as this new cultural awareness becomes embedded. With the transformation of the business we had defined and prepared for anything that was thrown at us. This was key; we didn't just talk about the changes that needed to happen, we project planned them, we communicated them, and we got buy-in for them.

Cheryl: What are some of the exciting outcomes you have achieved as a result of implementing the many changes in your strategic direction?

Josh/Gary: The most exciting outcome was the rise of the hidden treasures—all of the people that you would have rated as the A team became the A+ and that started to happen as a result of feeling like they were a vital part of the future of the company and they wanted to help everyone else to succeed. Everyone became "sharers," and we could not have done this without the A team. We were asking them to believe without being privy to the big strategic changes. Communicating and believing in the process—when changes occurred they were like "I can't believe this happened!" They couldn't believe that their input was creating change and then they went to fear of "how." They were worried that they didn't have the experience to become this new version of being a performance-based company. It was a scary shift when we actually made the changes because we all jumped into a time of great uncertainty, but there was also a tremendous amount of excitement as we were all working toward building something new. People were forced to step up—and they did and that is exciting! We told them that we were taking care of the management/leadership problems and we are all now expected to do more. They rose to the occasion, now they *want* to do more because they see the changes, they trust that we will "walk our talk" and they want to be a part of a company that is leading transformation not just in the company but in the community. More exciting outcomes: seeing people that you thought may have had the capabilities but weren't able to because they were not given the opportunity or the autonomy, seeing people with tears of joy, being told thank you and those people stepping up and they are with you 100 percent. They understood the huge undertaking and the risks that we took—we really hung it all out there—we modeled taking a risk for the greater good. We did it for the company and the employees and because there were constraints that needed to be taken care of. Super excited at the buy in and so exciting to see a 15-year employee who never got to use the gifts and skills that he had all along. Exciting because now we hear, "How can I help?" and everyone is stepping up big time.

Cheryl: What do you find is the most challenging for the teams you lead as it relates to change of direction and identity of the company?

Gary/Josh: We still have lots of work to do; there is no end to this journey. One of the challenges is to remain focused on where we are going—we have the right attitudes—but there are continual business changes in products and services and a lot of learning and education. Our teams are now *living* ongoing change, and this is both a challenge and a great process of the company. For

(Continued)

example, we are opening and remodeled our main big office, which opens to the customer on April 1st, 2015. We knew that customer service would be nervous, and so we talked to customer service about their fears. We assured them that we are going to learn this together and we are going to do this together. The response from our customer service team was that they had tears in their eyes. When we asked why, they said, "You said 'we' instead of 'I' or 'you'." They knew we had their back. In the past, they would have been told alone and pressured and "sink or swim." We provide the support systems. The challenge is to continue to earn the trust and care of our employees as we drive transformation.

Cheryl: Why do you think it's so important for everyone on the team to buy in to the vision and what types of things do you do to keep all teams engaged with the vision and the strategy?

Gary/Josh: We are only as strong as our weakest link. As you get people rising, they become influencers, and they become a model to the weaker links. The process of one-on-one communication is a continual activity and even with all of this we likely have some stragglers. We are focused on staying energetically engaged with teams to stay energized and focused on the goals and working together.

We meet with the teams regularly and we spend coaching time with key stakeholders and we provide situational support and coaching. We are about six months into our major change and there are still people with challenge of old habits and we are there to coach and remind them and engage them: asking them questions, encouraging them to ask questions and to come to us with a solution. The more we engage everyone the easier it is to create the necessary customer innovations. It is crucial to our momentum that we have begun.

Cheryl: What are the types of questions you ask yourselves and others as you lead this company change?

Josh/Gary: How can we streamline and increase efficiencies—engage them for the solutions and part of the future?

We are teaching our employees to ask "better" questions such as:

How can we be the best in customer care in our industry?
How can I bring creative solutions to this problem?
How can I be even more of a team player?

Cheryl: Moving forward what do you think are the opportunities for businesses *overall* as it relates to changing to meet market demands?

Gary/Josh: Senior-team synergy—you need teams that are excited to work with each other; you need teams who are able to work together and working with someone who has the knowledge with the right mind-set.

There is no room for ego only contribution of energy and ideas.

When you are on a great team, there is no ego because the *team* is great not the individuals, moving from a hierarchy to a shared leadership focus.

Involve your employees in your strategies and decisions, for example we sent out a survey asking our employees for the top attributes that they wanted to see for the person we would hire in a new position. We knew we had the right guy, but we did the survey to have the employees identify

(Continued)

the attributes; then we could say "you" helped choose this guy and *this* increased commitment to work together.

Cheryl: Transformation is ongoing. What's next for you?

Josh/Gary: We really want to build on the fact that we are a company that we want to be now *and* we want to leverage the unified team approach of the company to elevate our sales and service. We have the right people in place to now help us educate the customers, create new solutions, and to diversify the business. We want to thank you, Cheryl, as you were the catalyst as the consultant that helped us set the company direction, outline the strategic direction, and built us an actual project plan that we then implemented.

The interview with Josh and Gary really demonstrates the incredible mind-set that they have as senior leaders, and, in addition, they put in the structures and actions necessary to transform their business along with their entire team of employees in the company.

They both demonstrated that they indeed hacked the status quo and took the necessary actions toward transformation. Change on its own can be viewed as disruptive, and it's HOW leaders view the disruption and what they do about it that creates a new level of success for all.

4

Upgrade the Leadership OS to Be a Change Leader Who Drives Transformation

Life is like a 10-speed bicycle. Most of us have gears we never use.

—Charles M. Schulz

I n a Global Outlook Survey completed in 2015, a survey question asked which sector was most trusted in leadership. The responses were:

- Nonprofit and charitable organizations
- Business
- Education
- International organizations
- Healthcare

News media, government, and religious groups were ranked the lowest. The results of this survey clearly show that the general public can identify the levels of trust they have with various sectors. The need for transformation in each sector and industry is higher than ever before.

The survey went on to ask what change leadership skills are required to win back confidence and trust. The skills identified as needed are:

- Global interdisciplinary perspective
- Long-term planning
- Strong communication skills
- Prioritization of social justice and well being over financial growth
- Empathy, courage, morality, and a collaborative nature

The type of leader that emerges from the skills identified as needed is a leader who has an upgraded leadership operating system. The upgraded leadership system is a mind-set that shifts away from creating polarity or competition and moves toward creating *coopetition* (a blend of competition and cooperation) and integrative solutions. The new upgraded leadership operating system mind-set unifies the ability to inspire with the ability to mediate, to build mutually acceptable solutions, and it is inclusive of others' ideas and opinions prior to making a final decision.

This new mind-set requires flexibility and a willingness to stay focused on the benefit for all rather than "each man or woman for himself or herself."

How do we upgrade the leadership operating system?

With awareness, training, and practice.

In a recent *Business Insider* article futurist Faith Popcorn predicts a pretty far-out future. Popcorn is the same futurist who predicted the work-from-home and the free-agent-nation phenomena that have been going on for the past decade. Her predictions for 2025 include: technology will no longer be a tool but actually a part of us. That's right! Microchips embedded into the human body is a truly upgraded operating system. If that prediction makes you feel as if you are in the movie *Minority Report* or *The Matrix*, you are not alone.

With the prediction of implanted microchips, where does that take your thoughts? Do you immediately go to a negative thought like "no way am I doing that" or do you go to curiosity thinking such as "that could be cool" or do you immediately go to "sign me up!"

A new upgraded leadership operating system allows you, as a change leader, to make the leap from any form of resistance to action and to faster response rates to change. It allows you to go from thinking "not me" to "sure, let's check this out!" in a much faster time frame than previously achieved.

Trendwatchers and other futurists have also confirmed Popcorn's prediction—just look at children today (who are the future workers of the new workplace). They are learning at school on tablets and personal devices; they are connecting globally with students worldwide using touch technology, and they are innately leveraging technology as an integrated part of who they are. When I wrote my book on generations, *101 Ways to Make Generations, X, Y and Zoomers Happy at Work*, the research at that time confirmed that technology would be the true differentiator in the workplace. The generation known as Generation Z (those who are 20 and under) are completely integrating technology solutions with being human, and I often say, if you are afraid of Generation Ys (those in their 20s to early 30s)—be very afraid of Generation Zs!

The upgraded operating system that I am referring to here in this book does not involved implanting microchips, although at the time of the writing of this book, the Apple Watch has just been released.

Popcorn also predicts that by the year 2025 robots will have replaced one-third of the working population. She goes on to say that this will allow people to work in multiple jobs (similar to a consultant) in multiple industries and mostly from home. What do you think has to happen to the flexibility of thought in order to be completely adaptive to a robot reality and a reality in which human workers work for multiple companies in multiple jobs?

We need to have upgraded leadership operating systems (mind-sets) *now* in order to be flexible and resourceful, because these major technological and workplace structure changes become part of our future reality.

THE NEW LEADERSHIP OPERATING SYSTEM NEEDS EVOLVING CONSCIOUS THOUGHT PROCESSES

So how do you go from the level of evolutionary thought processes you have now to a mastery level of thought that becomes the cornerstone of the new leadership operating system?

To affect change that drives transformation, the leader (you) needs to transform self.

One of the least discussed leadership competencies, self-awareness, is possibly one of the most valuable. Self-awareness is being conscious of your thoughts, your perspectives, and your impact on others.

Self-awareness from an upgraded leadership operating system has evolved to multiple-perspectives awareness.

Earlier I mentioned Dr. Epstein and his evolutionary programs that help human beings to personally transform through unique health applications. One of the primary concepts he discusses in his lectures is to use the triple-A approach.

The triple-A approach stands for:

Awareness
Acknowledgment
Acceptance

In order to shift to where you are now and to go to where you want to be, you must first become aware of what is working, what needs to be changed, and what the opportunities are for change. For example, you may be fully aware that your thought patterns as they are now may not be supporting what you want to create, *and* you may not know what to do with this level of awareness. Or you may not have current conscious awareness of how you may be blocking progress.

Have you ever experienced those situations in which you know that if you say the same things you have always said before to certain people that absolutely nothing is going to change? In other words you have full awareness that you are engaged in a pattern that always ends up the same way. You know the saying, "If you want to get what you have always gotten then do what you have always done"? Well that is true for your operating system, too. You could choose to keep your thoughts exactly the same as they have been and you will continue to create the same results. With the commitment to upgrade your leadership operating system you are willing to become more aware of your thoughts and to "take a different street." There is a Tibetan proverb that goes like this:

Chapter one: I walk down the street. There is a hole in the sidewalk. I fall in.

Chapter two: I walk down the street. There is a hole in the sidewalk. I fall in.

Chapter three: I walk down the street. There is a hole in the sidewalk. I see it and I fall in.

Chapter four: I walk down the street. There is a hole in the sidewalk. I see it and I walk around it.

Chapter five: I take another street!

This proverb is a great metaphor for change: how many times do you go through the same situations with the same people and end up with the same outcomes? It is because someone, namely you, has to make the decision to take a different street. That is in essence what I am referring to when sharing the concept of upgrading the leadership operating system. In order to deal with the fast pace of change and to be flexible and adaptable leaders of change, you need to think differently.

I just had a call with a CEO coach client. We were talking about the challenges she was having with a certain leader on her team, and she was really struggling with her thoughts. She had gone from having complete confidence in her leader to feeling as if she had lost confidence in the leader. I was able to help her identify that it was her thoughts that created the perception that perhaps this leader was no longer valuable to the team. We worked on increasing her awareness around the patterns that she and the leader engage in that end up in confusion and lack of clarity. The patterns include the thoughts that she had previously about the leader and the thoughts that she was repeating even though there was no evidence for her losing-confidence thoughts. With a series of questions, I was able to help her identify that the person she had lost confidence in was actually herself. Her lack of confidence in herself caused her to feel insecure, which then caused her to have thoughts of doubt and negativity about the leader she was challenged with.

Once she was able to grasp an awareness of how her thoughts were actually creating the repeat pattern that she had with this person, she was able to quickly shift into new thoughts. Her thoughts went from, "This leader is not capable to do his role" to "I need to clarify and shift my thoughts to include a multiple perspective approach." The ability to hold a multiple perspective approach is a new thought strategy that is part of the upgraded leadership operating system.

Many leaders have developed the ability to see it from the other person's point of view and a multiple-perspectives approach goes beyond that ability.

The multiple-perspectives approach includes the ability to hold awareness of self and one's own thoughts while being able to also hold awareness and insight into others thoughts while holding the overall bigger picture of all factors in the mind at the same time.

Let me give you an example with the CEO I mentioned earlier: in the current mind-set the CEO was holding her own perspective while forgetting to include the mind-set of the other leader as well as the overall bigger picture context. After she and I had our coach call, she messaged me back to let me know that she had used the multiple perspectives approach when she met with the leader and she was amazed at how it quickly and easily moved the relationship forward and set a new standard for interaction for her and the other leader. She went on to explain that she thought more about what the leader was dealing with, how he communicates, what his current challenges were, what his priorities were, and at the same time she was able to factor in the bigger picture of what was going on in the company so that, when she reached out to the leader again, she was able to sincerely apologize for her approach, she was able to validate the other leader's contributions, and focus on the context of how both she and the other leader are focused on the same outcome, which is to move the business forward.

How do you leverage the skill of the multiple perspectives approach?

You practice daily giving awareness to your thoughts: are your thoughts adding value as in moving you toward a more energized state or are they causing you worry, anxiety, or doubt?

For the next few weeks when alone or when with others, notice your thoughts—are you thinking mostly about yourself?

Monitor your thoughts—are you including the thoughts and feelings of others and taking that into your overall thinking processes when dealing with others?

When your thoughts are negative or focused on what's wrong rather than what's right, catch yourself and look for thoughts that help you shift into looking at the bigger picture.

The key is being aware of where you are when you check in to monitor your thoughts.

Affirm your thoughts, whatever they are; by becoming aware of where you are, you can make the shift to change.

When you are feeling frustrated, first be aware that in that moment you are frustrated—be with it—and then notice it shift into the next thought.

When you are feeling angry—be aware that you are feeling angry and then notice it shift into the next thought.

The next step is acknowledgment of your thoughts and being with the acknowledgment. This is different than becoming aware. Awareness is when you are bringing your thoughts into the attention of your mind; acknowledgment is when you are willing to be with the thoughts and you are able to move toward acceptance. Acceptance is when you take full responsibility for the outcomes that your thoughts have created, and once you fully accept them, you are able to then choose a new and different "street."

The multiple perspectives approach is a key strategy for upgrading to a new leadership operating system.

Dr. David Hawkins is the author of a favorite book of mine: *The Eye of the I.* In it he describes the different levels of energy that come with different thoughts and emotions. Apathy is lower energy than anger, and anger is better than depression. It's an excellent book on building awareness about the energy and power of thoughts/emotions. I created a model that simply identifies the energy that comes with four different levels or filters as it relates to leadership. It is called the four levels of leadership awareness.

As you can see in Figure 4.1, it is an upward moving model that is a tool for increasing awareness about which level you may be at and for using the model to shift to the next level.

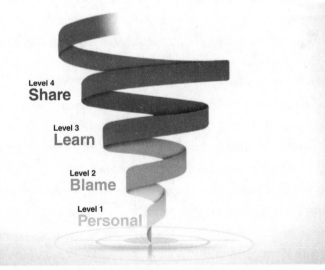

Figure 4.1   Four Levels of Leadership Awareness

Level 1 is Personal: When someone is at the personal level his or her thoughts are, "Why me?" or "Why am I the only one?" or "How come no one else does this as good as me?" You feel alone, immobilized, and possibly even depressed at this level.

These thoughts are low energy and create constriction and tension and the language while in this level will likely be condescending, critical, and judgmental. I know that readers of this book do not spend a lot of time here and yet as humans we all cycle through these levels. The goal is to spend the majority of our time in level 3 or 4.

Level 2 is Blame: When someone is at the blame level, it's a little bit better than taking things personally because the emotion that goes with level two is anger. However, it is still low energy because it's about powerlessness. The thoughts are, "It's not my fault, it's my bosses fault" or "It's not my fault, it's the government's fault" or "It's not my fault, it's my parents' fault." At this level you feel frustrated, not responsible, and typically irritated. The language at this level is accusatory, CYA, and defensive. The challenge with this level is that you are focused on power being outside your control. Once you are aware of being in levels 1 and 2, you can choose to shift to level 3.

Level 3 is Learn: At the level of learn, there is a huge energy release. At this level your thoughts are, "What can I learn from this situation or person?" or "What am I supposed to understand as a result of this situation or person?" or "How can I take what has worked in the past and apply it here while envisioning a new and successful outcome in this situation or with this person?" At level 3 you have integrated becoming aware, acknowledging your power to choose where you will be, and accepting the realities as they are while focusing on being a lifelong learner rather than a victim, which is level 1 or 2. The power of being in level 3 is immense, and then there is the extreme power of level 4.

Level 4 is Share: In level 4 it's as if you are Neo in *The Matrix.* When you are consistently choosing to be learning in level 3 you then see the value and the merits of consistently adding value, which is level 4, share. Your thoughts in level 4 are, "How can I share what I know to help this other person grow?" or "How can we share our ideas to come up with a better solution for all?" or "How can I add even more value to my team so that they are even more effective?" At level 4, you have recognized the immense energy that is available for collaboration, idea sharing, and sharing of resources. When you are at level 4, it is less about ego and more about being focused on multiple-perspective reality of creating good for the overall vision and for all involved. Personally, at level 4 you feel alive, you feel connected, you feel on purpose, and you feel as if you are contributing your gifts at the highest level possible.

The four-level leadership model is an excellent tool to help you become aware, to accept where you are and where others are, and to acknowledge (which is the same as taking responsibility) and to consciously choose to upgrade your leadership operating system.

THE NEW LANGUAGE OF THE NEW LEADERSHIP UPGRADED OPERATING SYSTEM

In addition to the thoughts of a leader with upgraded leadership operating systems, there is a new language that is evolving. This new language shifts to an inspiring and energy-creating approach that increases energy for self and ultimately for others.

The language is evolving from autocratic to inclusive. Making the change from a mind-set of authority and power toward a mind-set of sharing successes and equalization of power is a big one.

The ability to lead with this new leadership language is required to inspire and engage today's workforce and to set the tone for the future workplace.

The new emerging language focuses on "we" and "our" and "shared success" and the language is focused on the future and solution. The upgraded operating system language is focused on "elevating" energy and connection for all. To ensure you are using this new language ask yourself the following question before speaking, before writing an email, before texting, or instant messaging: "Is what I am about to communicate focused on gain and benefit for all people involved?"

Another great question is, "How can I add more value to this person or situation?"

THE COMMUNICATION SKILLS OF A LEADER WITH AN UPGRADED OPERATING SYSTEM

In addition to the new language of the upgraded leadership operating system, there are other components of the leadership operating system that need to be upgraded. The master change leader has developed the ability to ask powerful questions about his or her own performance and listen to feedback in new and evolved ways.

Gather The Multiple Perspectives of Others to Self-Improve

360-degree feedback is a feedback process where your superior, your peers and direct reports, and sometimes customers evaluate you. You receive an analysis of how you perceive yourself and how others perceive you. It is a powerful tool for personal change because it focuses on improving behaviors and actions. It is just as powerful a tool for organizational change and development. 360 feedback can be used to spur internal change (i.e., cultural shifts) by involving all company stakeholders such as senior management, departments, teams, and individual employees. Companies benefit also from eliciting feedback from external audiences, such as customers, in order to better adapt to changing technology, trends, and expectations. Implementing a recurring cycle of feedback will give your organization a competitive advantage and allow you to continually improve your products and services.

As a leader, you may have participated in 360-degree feedback; whether you enjoyed the process will be dependent on how you perceive being evaluated as well as how well the process was facilitated. A leader with an upgraded leadership operating system not only welcomes feedback, he or she encourages it as being a key success factor in becoming a better leader. The skill of asking good questions can be invaluable to you to help you upgrade your leadership operation system. When the question is about your own performance, however, it can be harder to be objective about feedback. When you show that you are open to multiple perspectives of feedback, you demonstrate evolved self-awareness and the willingness to be open.

In addition, asking questions about your own performance models a transparent approach. Most importantly, it encourages everyone to see that it's fantastic for a master leader of change to be constantly learning and growing.

Regardless of whether you have a formal 360-degree performance system in place, you will want to gather ongoing feedback from your teams, your peers, and your employees to improve your performance and to upgrade your leadership operating system.

You can have people use the assessment that follows. You can copy and paste it into a SurveyMonkey format and gather the feedback anonymously. We often do this for the executives our team coaches, and we use it as part of the coaching format. It's one thing to know your own performance, it's another to have an evaluation from your boss, and it's extremely valuable to have multiple-perspective input on your approach so that you can use it as a tool to upgrade your leadership operating system.

Change Leadership Assessment—360-Degree Feedback: Template

The following assessment is to be used as a tool to gather multiple perspectives on my performance as your leader as it relates to change and transformation. Please answer honestly and with as much constructive feedback and examples as possible.

> Question 1: On a scale of 1–10, with 10 being high, how would you rate me as a leader who leads change in an inspiring and visionary way?
>
> Question 2: On a scale of 1–10, with 10 being high, how would you rate me in my ability to adapt to market changes or customer influenced changes?
>
> Question 3: On a scale of 1–10, with 10 being high, how would you rate me in my ability to coach and guide you through change?
>
> Question 4: On a scale of 1–10, with 10 being high, how would you rate me as a leader that provides you with tools and resources?
>
> Question 5: On a scale of 1–10, with 10 being high, how would you rate me on my ability to facilitate solutions within the team?
>
> Question 6: On a scale of 1–10, with 10 being high, how would you rate me on my ability to communicate in a way that inspires you?

Question 7: What specific feedback do you have for me to help me be an even better leader?

Question 8: What specific feedback do you have for me to help you be even more effective in your role?

For your online version of a 360 degree template please go to www.cherylcran.com/360assessment.com.

If you have the courage to have your team and your peers or even your customers complete this assessment (you can edit the questions for the group you are surveying), then you will gain so much from hearing the feedback and using it as a tool to further upgrade your leadership operating system.

EMOTIONAL INTELLIGENCE: A TOOL FOR UPGRADING THE LEADERSHIP OPERATING SYSTEM

One of the most potent tools for a leader of change mastery is the ability to master emotional intelligence. Emotional intelligence is the ability to build awareness of your own emotional scale and then use that awareness to be able to relate to others' emotional states more easily.

When leading change you cannot underestimate the emotions that arise due to the psychological factors related to change. The typical reactions to ongoing and rapid change are fear, anxiety, and worry. Not only do you as a leader experience those emotions so does everyone in any organization. Believe it or not, the organizations that have leaders with the highest degrees of emotional intelligence have an organization that is more flexible and innovative.

University of California–San Francisco professors Lewis, Amini, and Lannon say in their book, A General Theory of Love, that emotions are at the root of everything we do. In all cases, emotions are humanity's motivator. The human brain consists of two brains, the limbic (emotional center) and the cortex (the higher level processor). The limbic system processes all the incoming data before the cortex or the logic side of the brain. The emotions control the context of information before it is passed on to the cortex.

Having emotional intelligence has been an overlooked or minimized skill. IQ, or intelligence based on the cortex, has been valued over the EQ, or emotional intelligence, which is based on the limbic. In truth it is the integration of both sides of the brain that creates the new upgraded operating system I am talking about in this chapter.

When you understand the power of emotions as it relates to leading change and you learn to use emotional intelligence as an added skill, you are rewiring the brain.

The power of emotions can shift solutions. In a *Harvard Review* blog by Peter Bregman titled, "A Story about Motivation," he provides a great example of understanding the power of emotions and identity. He shares a situation in which AARP (American Association of Retired Persons) asked some lawyers if they would reduce their fee to $30 an hour to help needy retirees. The request was made without any honoring of the ego or the emotional reaction a lawyer may have to that request. The result: the lawyers said no. The leadership at AARP gave it some thought and came back to the lawyers asking if they would do it for free and volunteer their time. The lawyers came back with a unanimous yes. Why?

The first request appeared to diminish the value of the lawyers' time and identity. The second request when asked as a favor appealed to the emotional reality of the lawyer asking himself or herself a question, "Am I the kind of person who helps people in need?" Versus the question "Am I the kind of person who works for a reduced fee of $30 an hour?"

The four components of emotional intelligence are self-awareness, social awareness, self-management, and relationship management. We talked earlier in this chapter about self-awareness and the new evolved version that is multiple-perspective awareness. In other previous sections of this chapter, we talked about components of self-management such as the 360-degree feedback and the language of a change leader that drives transformation. There are many ways to assess your emotional intelligence skills. I have facilitated EQ coaching for executives using the PEQM (Personal Emotional Quotient Meter) assessment. The assessment is taken with a special access code and the report that you receive provides a graph that shows the range of emotional intelligence in each of four quadrants. It also provides detailed overviews of how to improve each of the areas and guidelines for further development. For your access to taking your own PEQM or setting it up for your teams go to www.cherylcran.com/PEQM.

MINDFULNESS: A TOOL FOR UPGRADING THE LEADERSHIP OPERATING SYSTEM

Finally, the tool that is becoming more and more popular for increasing the ability to be adaptive to change is mindfulness. Organizations in Silicon Valley have been participating in mindfulness training for the past few years, and companies in Europe have been early adopters of the training as well.

Mindfulness is an awareness tool to become more present with thoughts, build awareness of stress reactions, and help you accept where you are so that you can move forward with ease.

In this age of smartphones, instant messaging, and 24/7 availability, leaders find that it is increasingly difficult to find time to step away and connect with one's self. The reality is that the technological age is creating a deeper need to "reset" and "reconnect" with self in a nontech way.

There is no need for a gadget to meditate; all you need is access to your operating system where your resource is pre-installed in you.

Technology is being used in some meditation and mindfulness trainings, and trainers are using technology in interesting ways. The mindfulness tools range from meditation timers to full meditation programs.

Trainings in mindfulness practices have become the norm at some of Silicon Valley's signature tech giants such as Google, Apple, Twitter, and others.

There is a tremendous desire in Silicon Valley for tools to help calm and slow down the mind as everyone there is addicted to speed. The initial reaction of people in the first couple of mindfulness sessions is that there's not much of anything to it. Well-known meditation teacher Kabat-Zinn says:

> We're so conditioned to doing, that we forget about the element of being human. So when we drop into being, it seems like, wait a minute, nothing's happening. I've got work to do, deadlines to meet. And you realize how driven we can become getting onto the next thing. If you do that your whole life, you just drop into your grave and you haven't actually lived.

I have been a student of mindfulness practice for over 20 years and when I started I could barely sit still. Today being able to be still and meditate as well as use other mindful practices such as yoga or other body focused mindfulness practices is what I call my secret weapon in these times of super-fast-paced change.

There are a number of apps that can help you practice mindfulness available at Mindfulnessapps.com. You can find related tools at Mindfulnesshealth.com. In addition I have mindfulness practices that have been incorporated into programs that I have co-created with Dr. Epstein, and I will share more about those later in this book.

In his biography on Steve Jobs, author Walter Isaacson shares how mindfulness was a tool that Jobs relied on. In addition to Jobs, Salesforce CEO Marc Benioff and LinkedIn CEO Jeff Weiner regularly practice mindfulness too. They and other top leaders meditate, and they claim mindfulness and meditation as a factor in their success.

Even Wall Street is leveraging meditation/mindfulness as a tool. Ray Dalio of Bridgewater Associates claims that "meditation more than anything in my life was the biggest factor in whatever success I've had."

The upgrading of the leadership operating system involves a new way of thinking, a new set of habits, a new way of being, and a new commitment to focusing on self-leadership first. The new operating system guides leaders to be more open, more honest, more transparent, and more connected to self and, therefore, to others.

To recap the chapter, there is a need for a new way of leading the self and this requires new thoughts, a willingness to be evaluated and to continue to learn and grow. A new operating system also includes increasing emotional intelligence and using tools to slow down the mind in order to be faster and more responsive to fast and unrelenting paces of change.

And there are (r)evolutionary new programs that also aid in upgrading the operating system such as those that focus on "energy" as THE resource of the future and now. I share more of these in the chapters that follow.

5

The Change Cycle
Transformation Tool

If you get the culture right, most of the other stuff will take care of itself.

—Tony Hsieh, CEO Zappos

In Chapter 4 we focused on the importance of being a flexible and adaptable change leader with an upgraded operating system. Upgrading the leadership operating system is a key component of being able to successfully navigate self and others through change.

In this chapter we will look at the change cycle model and how to use it for leading change for self, others and for the organization.

Think about a recent big change in your own life. Maybe it was a job change, a relationship-status change, a new baby, someone passed away, someone had a health crisis, reaching a milestone birthday. Each of these are changes that impact our lives. Typically it is easier to accept a perceived positive change than a perceived negative change. I say "perceived" because truly it is the lens with which we look at something that determines how we respond to it. A milestone birthday may be super exciting for someone and absolutely painful for someone else.

A lot of how we each process change is dependent on how we think about the change. This is why I suggest that we all need to upgrade our operating systems because we can rewire the brain to be more adaptable and creative rather than relying on the typical flight-or-fight reaction that most people use when faced with major change. The change cycle model in Figure 5.1 shows the stages of change and the thinking and behavior that goes along with each stage.

In the process visual I have created, there are six distinct elements in the cycle of change, and each cycle brings its own unique nuances that affect the self, others, and business. Many fail to recognize or deal with the realities of psychological responses to change, and this can be detrimental to the people and the business overall.

Next we look at the progression and impact of the six elements of change as outlined in Figure 5.1.

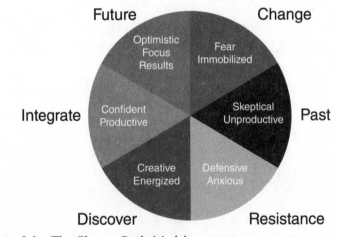

Figure 5.1   The Change Cycle Model

CHANGE

When the change happens (this can be ongoing change or rapid change or both) the typical initial reaction/response is fear. There are different reactions and each reaction is caused by different concerns that include reactions that are outlined in the following sections.

Bewilderment and Confusion and the Need to Ask Questions

When people get over the initial shock or surprise of a change, the first initial reaction is often to ask questions, which fills the need to find out why something is happening and to rationalize or better understand the "why."

Depending on how the questions are answered, the people who are reacting may or may not feel that they can trust or that they are being told the right information. The reason most people ask questions is to form opinions about the safety of the change and to give it personal meaning.

Questions are asked also to seek assurance of support or fairness to self and others. People feel that if they cannot change what happens, at least they feel that they should be treated fairly and with respect. Organizational-change leaders who use perceived fair approaches and processes are able to make far greater changes, more successfully, than others.

When you are the one on the receiving end of questions due to a change, the questions being asked are a very useful window into the other person's thoughts and state of mind. Listen for the needs behind the questions. Be compassionate and patient with the concerns. Answer the concerns with truth, honesty, and care. This will give you, the change leader, the starting point of being able to begin helping people to see the value of the change and to help them take a change leader approach to the change itself.

The Need to Understand the Impact of Change on People

As interconnected beings, people will also seek to understand how the changes and the effects of the changes impact other people. There will be concern about the well-being of friends and colleagues. People may be feeling guilty because they are not adversely affected by the change but that others with whom they work are. People may engage in politics in order to protect their jobs. The behaviors connected with this reaction are often gossip, backstabbing, choosing teams, on the negative side. Other positive behaviors connected with this reaction may include supporting, coaching, and guiding others.

Years ago when I was working for a mortgage insurance company, we were downsized across the country to reduce our employee base by 50 percent. The company was filing for Chapter 11 and needed to reorganize rapidly. I was an area manager at the time and I was asked to stay to help manage the transition. I felt incredibly guilty because people I had worked with who had been with the company many years more than me were being packaged out. My response to the change was to support and help those who were leaving by helping them find new jobs, get support with the job search, and align them with networks to support their efforts. I do remember though feeling sad, guilty, and nonproductive for a period of time during the transition. I lasted three months managing the transition, and then I went to my boss at the time and gave my letter of resignation. I could not manage the change the way they wanted me to, which was to continue to assure those who were still with the company that they would have jobs when I knew that they would not. That experience for me was a lesson in how *not to do* a major change.

Knee-Jerk Reactions. Some people when threatened by a change, especially if there is a high risk impact such as the loss of a job, will immediately update their resumes and begin looking for a job elsewhere. A knee-jerk reaction involves jumping ship too rapidly when faced with a change before gathering data and assessing the risks and potentials of a change situation. The reason for this is a form of personal protection. This is an important time to ensure that you as an individual have all the information you can access so that you don't make a rush decision to leave before its time. From a change-leader standpoint this is a vulnerable time where you could lose your top performers if you do not focus on keeping them engaged and informed throughout the change situation. In my preceding story at the mortgage insurance company, I waited three months before making the decision to leave. I talked daily with my boss Donna, and when I did decide to leave, it was after I had assessed that I had helped my team members and evaluated my options.

Noncommittal Reactions. Another approach people will take is to keep their heads down and keep their fingers crossed that they are not noticed. They will try to not rock the boat, they will attend meetings, but when they are asked for an opinion (which they will always seek to avoid anyway), they will make noncommittal answers for fear of bringing attention to themselves. They use the fingers-crossed hope that when managers are looking for people to cut, they will pass this person by as a solid and useful worker.

Leading-Change Reactions. The leading-change reaction is to be a part of the solution rather than a part of the problem. The people leading the change, join in all of the activities and do whatever is asked of them. They are supporters and collaborators. They are focused on being creative and on the future as well as providing resources that help everyone as they navigate the change.

The leading-change reaction is your clue about who your influencers will be. You want to leverage these people throughout the change cycle.

PAST

This is the next phase in the change cycle. Once the change has occurred, people experience the change by attaching to the past and how things have been done before. Some people will romanticize the past and want to protect the past because it was more favorable to him or her personally. Some of the behaviors of those who focus on the past are to either unconsciously or consciously sabotage the future change initiative. Often the behavior can be passive-aggressive when the focus is on protecting the past. The master change leader will recognize that the past holds success stories and value as a reference point for where the team and the organization have been. In addition, the past holds information of failure and success that can be used to help guide the change initiative. Bridging the past into the change of the present and the future is a skill and a technique that advanced change leaders leverage. I will share more about this later in the book as a unique evolutionary approach to ensuring a greater group buy-in by using a past/future approach that increases success change processes.

RESISTANCE

The next phase in the change cycle is resistance to the changes, which are different than the change reactions. A number of people as mentioned earlier, have an attachment to how things were done in the past. Others may challenge the veracity of the changes and their validity; they may think that the change does not make sense or that not enough research was done, or they may simply disagree with various elements of the change initiative, which can lead to anxiety and defensive behaviors. Resistance to change is an emotional and behavioral response by the affected employees to real or imagined threats to an established work routine. Organizations must lead change and any resistance that arises.

There are a number of reasons that people will resist and they include the following.

Fear of Failure

People will resist change because of the fear of failure. Fast changing and big structural and cultural changes can cause a person to doubt their capabilities. Fear of failure can increase self-doubt and diminish self-confidence. When someone has a fear of failure it undermines his or her personal growth and development. This fear will also cause a person to oppose changes without considering the potential benefits of the proposed changes. The art of a change leader is to be a cheerleader, to recognize the resistances, and to mitigate them in advance.

Loss of Status or Hierarchy

The fear of loss of status comes from the ego. People become attached to the identity of their job or their position. When there are structural and cultural changes that threaten to change the people's powerful position or job it will generally trigger strong resistance. Often, corporate restructuring and reorganization may involve elimination of managerial jobs. People will resist restructuring and any other program that reduces their authority and the status they already enjoy in the organization. The change leader can mitigate this resistance by openly communicating the impact on current status and future status and helping to paint a vision of collaboration and opportunity for the future.

No Apparent Rewards

Individuals resist when they cannot see immediate positive rewards for changing their work routines. People want to see a positive improvement in their work in order to readily accept change. An employee is less likely to support a change that does not address the impact on workload or resources. A change leader needs to factor in this resistance when building the change strategy with the team—rewards need to be built into the change initiative. The master change leader needs to also openly provide access to resources and support throughout the change.

Organizational Culture Norms

Another type of resistance is the reluctance to go against the common culture or norms of the company. Every company has its own organizational norm or culture. There are established rules, both spoken and unspoken, within the company. The norms of the culture may be in complete opposition to the changes being introduced. Groups develop and enforce conformity to a set of norms that guide the members' behavior. However, conformity to *existing* group norms may discourage employees from accepting future organizational change. The established norms that conflict with the desired changes need to be addressed and brought out in the open, whereas the structural and cultural norms that work to improve the organization need to be positively promoted by the change leaders.

Changing Routine Patterns

The last form of resistance is the one that most people struggle with which is to give up doing what they have become accustomed to doing. People are creatures of habit and find it difficult to abandon repetitive tasks and routines that the organization considers no longer appropriate. Generally, people like their comfort zones. People tend to resist structural and cultural changes that force them out of their comfort zones. The new change requires investing more time and energy to learn new role patterns. The art of a change leader who is leading through this resistance is to provide compelling reasons that the new approach will be more effective, will save time, will produce new results, and will help the people learn and grow.

DISCOVER

The phase after resistance begins the point at which the energy being exerted by the change leader is less about putting out fires and keeping people focused, and more about harnessing the willingness of people to move forward. At this point, everyone realizes that the change is or was inevitable, and they accept that it has happened, and they then become energized and creative about the possibilities. I mentioned in Chapter 4 about the power of the Triple-A approach: awareness, acknowledgment, and acceptance. In the discover phase, the majority of people involved in the change have moved into acceptance. Now that there is acceptance, there is a unified sigh of relief and a desire to learn and grow. The behaviors in the discover phase include: noticing personal behavior and identifying when people are in change/reaction and resistance, taking responsibility for responses to the change and the impact of behavior on others, asking questions that are focused on future and solutions, and investigating the opportunities that the new change brings for self and others. A change leader harnesses the energy-valve release of the discover phase and focuses on ensuring the team stays focused on this stage, and catches people when they slide into resistance or reaction. When change leaders see individuals moving backward from discover, they provide coaching, resources, and cheerleading to keep the majority of the team focused on moving forward with the changes.

INTEGRATE

The next stage has even higher energy because the majority of the team has now been integrated. The change leader has provided guidance to help individuals develop a skill set that includes self-organizing skills for each person such as personal awareness, change-leadership approach, the change cycle as a transformation tool, and personal accountability. With continual communication by the change leader, the team begins to integrate the past; overcome resistance; feel creative and energized, which leads them to feeling confident and productive. The integrate phase is where everyone has not only bought into the change but they also are personally invested in creating a positive future and driving transformation forward. The change leader has invested his or her time with each individual to help them overcome resistance, to build skills that increase adapt-ability and to be leaders of change themselves. The behaviors of individuals in the integrate phase are: brainstorming creative solutions, working together as a team, and supporting each other to be successful; they are less about ego and more about creat-ing the positive changes for the benefit of all, focused on growth and learning and finding resources and tools that help the teams and the organization overall.

FUTURE

The last phase of the change cycles is the future phase. With the integration phase complete and most of the team on board, the team is now completely future focused, optimistic, and getting new results. In the future phase, the focus is purely on maximiz-ing the strategy and the goals of the new plan for the future. The majority of the team is on board and the change leader identifies his or her influencers or the change leaders who are demon-strating the integration of the change cycle on a personal level. The change leader empowers the change leaders to be cheer-leaders, coaches, and resources to the team. The change leader drives the strategy for change while ensuring that the people are receiving constant communication, milestone updates on the progress of the change, and are being excitedly reminded of the compelling future. The behaviors of those in the future phase of the cycle include consistently inspiring and bringing humor and energy to the team, always looking for the signs of anyone who is negating the change efforts by falling back into resistance, and instantly providing coaching and support to the entire team.

The change cycle is ongoing and everyone goes around the cycle at varying rates of speed. The level that people adapt is related to their personality style, their past experiences with change, and their generational demographic. The change cycle is like a wheel; the art of change leadership is recognizing that the wheel is constantly turning and as a change initiative is achieved there are new changes that are going to begin the cycle again. As change leaders master the art of change, the cycle becomes easier and easier to navigate and there is less time spent in resistance and more time spent in discover and integrate.

The change cycle model is a valuable change-leadership tool. As a change leader you would want to first evaluate yourself about where you are on the change cycle right now. If you are willing to admit that you are on the right side of the cycle meaning change, past, or resistance, you can then use the tools of awareness to shift yourself into the left side of the cycle.

Depending on what is going on in your world right now, both personally and professionally, you will find yourself at times moving quickly and easily to the discover, integrate, and future side of the change cycle. At other times you may stay longer than you would like in the change, past, or resistance of the change cycle.

In order to get others up to speed, you need to include them in the principles of change management and coach them with the skills to self-regulate and adapt to ongoing change.

Here are some questions to ask with regard to adapting to change and engaging your team members to adapt to change as well.

- Where am I right now on the change cycle?
- How am I behaving while I am in this stage?
- Am I stuck in this stage? Why?
- What can I do to shift myself out of this stage to the next?

- Where is each of my team members on the change cycle?
- How is this affecting their performance?
- Have I coached each of my team members on how to deal with ongoing change?
- Am I being consistent in coaching my team members through the cycle of change?

These questions are very helpful to help recognize the emotional and psychological aspects to dealing with change. Often, we underestimate our own process when it comes to dealing with challenges. More often, we underestimate the process of our team members and how each of them deals with the dynamics of change in unique ways.

EACH CYCLE HAS ITS PURPOSE AND IS PART OF THE TRANSFORMATION PROCESS

There is a purpose to each phase of the cycle, and each phase helps to progress the movement of the change forward.

I recently had the privilege of interviewing Duncan of Air Canada who is vice president of global sales. In the interview, I asked Duncan to explain how he used elements of the change cycle to create a massive transformation of operations that is revolutionizing customer care and employee engagement within the world class airline.

Interview with Duncan Bureau, VP of Global Sales, Air Canada

Cheryl: As a successful executive how did you develop your personal operating system as a change leader of transformation?

(*Continued*)

Duncan: I came from the West Jet environment where the focus was/is to look after employees, and when we look after employees they look after customers. The model was that West Jet is an organization of capitalists, which means that employees are paid for performance. It is ingrained that it is a culture of opportunity not entitlement. My focus as a leader has developed from that environment and a strong belief that we lose as a team and win as a team. With the pay-for-performance model, productivity and improvement are tied to a vested interest for each employee to being financially successful. It is easy to create a culture that is entrepreneurial and change savvy when employees are paid for how they contribute to the company growth. Here at Air Canada, under the leadership of our CEO Calin Rovenescu, there has been active focus on changing the culture to a performance-based culture and reward for performance. A culture of pay for performance is working in that Air Canada has had the best financial results in its 77-year history.

We have record volume, record profit, and this is due to a large shift in the mind-set of one team in Air Canada.

Cheryl: When you joined Air Canada what was your approach to get everyone on board quickly with your team approach?

Duncan: The first thing I did was look at the team we had in place and assess who was eager to be part of the compelling future, and we did make initial personnel changes. We created a team based on the brought forward philosophy from West Jet of "we lose as a team and we win as a team" and the new team consisted of talented people both internally and externally. We created a team by bringing in people who weren't handcuffed by historical thinking and who had high levels of entrepreneurial mindedness and accountability. A very important skill set that every person on the team must have is the ability to make decisions. My leadership motto is, make decisions—fail early and move on. This was a big change for many people in the culture as many were still entrenched in the previous culture of decisions coming from the top down. We pay people because of their ability to make decisions and judgments and, historically, the employees believed they were not able to make decisions. What I have found and our success shows that when front-line employees make customer-service decisions it's a better outcome for individuals (empowerment) and organizations (profits).

Cheryl: With the change to move to empowering front-line staff to make decisions what is/was the ultimate outcome?

Duncan: When I was at West Jet our experience was that our front-line employees were more frugal than executive would be. This was fascinating because, at the executive level, we would simply say, "Give the customers what what they want generously," when, in fact, because the employees/shareholders were on the ground and were the ones participating in the situation, they might deduce that the problem might be better solved with a Starbucks coffee and an apology. When all staff are shareholders they take the responsibility for the business very personally and it helps them to make informed and prudent decisions. We believe that when we spend and invest wisely and make a customer happy and make a decision the customer/guest is happy and employees feel like an integral part of the company and want to make a difference.

(Continued)

Cheryl: How does Air Canada use surveys as a way to monitor what is working and what changes need to be made?

Duncan: We do Air Canada engagement surveys on a regular basis. When I started at Air Canada I looked through the previously conducted surveys and found that a lot of people were not engaged. Also, I was getting e-mails from leaders to make a decision that could have been made at the local level. There had not been an active focus on giving decision-making power to the three or four levels below me. We began to help our employees change their mind-sets and to think and act like owners and do what's right—and then we would compensate them like owners. Air Canada has undergone massive change and transformation in the past five years and continues to focus on being a customer-focused culture. Anecdotally I am hearing from others how much Air Canada has improved.

Cheryl: What is a major change that has happened that you think has transformed the culture at Air Canada?

Duncan: Our senior leadership teams are change leaders driving transformation. Calin has done an outstanding job of building the executive team and driving our transformation for customers and culture.

A major accomplishment is Air Canada's 10-year deal with the pilots. This is unprecedented with a union group and huge kudos to Ben Smith who was heavily involved with negotiations and between the union and the executive team was sat at the same table. Both Calin and Ben knew that having both groups sit at the table and be part of the agreement was crucial to the 10-year pilot agreement. This agreement has created stability and is a huge win on both the employee level and on a customer-service level. Each employee agreement we achieve provides greater value for our customers. We are actively seeking to reach more widespread agreements so that we can focus on adding value to both employees and our customers. Lufthansa is struggling with its rotating strikes due to lack of ability to come to an agreement, and this hinders customer experience. Our president is sitting at the table for all agreements in order to have open and direct dialogue, and this is contributing to our success with our agreements with our unions.

Cheryl: What are the biggest challenges right now?

Duncan: Our continued challenge is getting people to buy into the fact that they can make decisions. We are focusing on providing coaching and guidance on this. Since helping our teams to be decision-makers, turnaround time is much quicker than ever before. We are a performance-based company and, to prove it, recently Air Canada made a shift to incentive and pay for performance in all of our compensation packages. We are having success and we want to replicate 2015 because the employees have had a taste of success and profit and this has increased engagement and an attitude of "we are all in this together."

Cheryl: What are other changes you are leading?

Duncan: We are investing in coaching and guidance to help people to change the historical mind-set. There had not been as much invested in leadership coaching or training for quite some time. We recognize that we need to invest in training and support. We are looking at who is on our team and identifying the skills gaps. We have indexed against all sales organizations within

(Continued)

different organizations and we are investing in leadership training—making sure that every one is a leader and taking ownership at all levels. Every single director/manager is going through leadership training and sales training and it has really helped the entire organization. We are also focused on minimizing silos and sharing information across the company. We have weekly team calls with the entire team. We have a lot of smart people and everyone is engaged and involved.

We also created diverse teams with both external new hires and promotions from within, and this has increased diversity of thought as well as innovation.

Cheryl: It sounds like you are driving the transformation in Air Canada. Any additional comments?

Duncan: I came to Air Canada with a few goals and they include wanting to contribute to the company very quickly as well as a big goal of being a top place to work. We have lots to be proud of, and we have a lot more we want to excel at. Ultimately we want to create an organization with entrepreneur-minded employees, and we are well on our way.

As you can see from the interview with Duncan at Air Canada, he is indeed a change leader. He has integrated the elements of the change cycle and is focused on keeping all team members focused on future and solution. The interview is a great example of a change leader moving through the change cycle and transformation tool and having strategy and consistent focus on adding value to customers and employees.

6

Help Lead Others to Be Change Leaders Who Drive Transformation

Culture does not change because we desire to change it.
Culture changes when the organization is transformed;
the culture reflects the realities of people working together
every day.

—Frances Hesselbein

The change cycle that I shared in Chapter 5 is a tool for understanding where you are on the cycle and the value of becoming a change leader who focuses on learning, growing, and having an eye to the future. In this chapter we explore how you as a change leader can help others to be change leaders and how you can inspire others to be drivers of transformation while creating a culture of engaged change leaders. Helping others through the change cycle and coaching them to increase their capabilities as it relates to leading change is one of the most rewarding things you as a leader can do.

My leadership philosophy is that everyone is and can be a leader. I mentioned in a previous chapter that Zappos has embraced this concept and has gone to the holocracy model, in which teams of people work together with a shared leadership approach. In a recent blog post on March 19, 2015, futurist Jacob Morgan explores the phenomena of managerless companies. There is a shift afoot where organizations are looking at the everyone-is-a-leader concept literally and applying it to the business operations. Companies such as Morningstar Farms, Sun Hydraulics, Valve, Medium, and W.L. Gore have all gone this route. The industries mentioned include tech, food manufacturing, and retail.

From a change-leader perspective a managerless approach is a progressive way for the future to have all employees identify themselves as leaders; what it does is increase autonomy and responsibility for individuals. The managerless company also gets rid of hierarchy and rigidity of policy that prohibits the ability to move quickly and drive transformation rapidly in a fast-paced world. The motive behind the change to a managerless company is a desire for a flatter and nimbler organization. Companies like Tangerine (formerly ING Direct Canada) have managers, but they do not ascribe to hierarchy, that is, they don't focus on titles or roles internally. Whirlpool has also shifted away from traditional managerial roles by creating four different types of leadership, in which all employees at the company are considered leaders of some kind (for example, if you are an entry level or junior employee you may be called "a leader of self").

So if everyone *is* a leader and the message of this book—a change leader—it begs the question, are *change* leaders born or made? Yes to some degree some have a natural leadership aptitude and personality geared toward being a leader *and* for others leadership is developed and we can coach, support, provide resources, and build skills to create change leaders!

Leadership mastery is a skill that includes the abilities outlined in Chapter 2 and an integration of change-management skills with change leadership skills.

From the description I laid out for you in that chapter, you would likely infer that great change leaders are *made*.

Table 6.1 looks at the two theories around this as a starting point for creating and helping change leaders to drive transformation.

The summary of the two theories outlined in Table 6.1 is that those born with innate qualities such as charisma, influence, and relationships skills have an easier time than those who have to learn them. However, all leadership aptitudes *can be learned* with a commitment to lifelong learning and a desire to adhere to the theory that "everyone is a leader."

How do you as a change leader inspire and encourage everyone you lead and influence to become change leaders?

First you must model the attributes of a change leader yourself, you must be aware, acknowledge, and accept where you are in the change cycle personally. You must connect with and understand where others are on the change cycle; you must provide the skills, the coaching, and the resources to help others; and you must see the big picture of how a company of change leaders is a very different kind of company.

Table 6.1   Are Change Leaders Born or Made?

Change Leaders Are Born	Change Leaders Are Made
Some "trait" theorists believe that some people have in-born qualities and traits that make them better suited to lead.	Behavioral theorists believe that people can become great leaders through training, coaching, and experience.
Like a child born with natural aptitude for a musical instrument, or athletic ability, theorists believe that people born with innate leadership have a natural tendency to excel and will show these qualities early in life.	Like riding a bike, leadership can be learned by anyone. Theorists believe that exposure to leadership traits and skills, as well as providing an environment for practice and application, can lead to leadership mastery.

I recently conducted an interview with John Moriarity, a senior leader of a top performing financial company E3 Wealth. I met John at a financial conference where I was the keynote speaker talking about "Leading with 2020 Vision" where I shared insights on how the future of business was changing and the impact on the industry of financial services.

John was a speaker on a panel prior to my keynote, and I immediately recognized him as a fellow change leader who is driving transformation in his industry. In the interview for this book, John provided excellent modeling of how a change leader thinks, and he is an example of a change leader who has inherent skills as well as one who has gained advanced change leader skills through his commitment to lifelong learning.

This interview gives a glimpse into his mind-set and approach, and how his big vision to "change finance for all Americans" is what propels him forward. This interview also gives you a glimpse into the innate leadership qualities that John has as well as what he continues to "learn" in order to further develop his change leadership skills. He refers to his mentor Mark many times as the inspirational change leader who helped him shape his approach and ultimately his success.

Interview with John Moriarity, Founder and President of E3 Wealth

Cheryl: John, thank you for your time today. Can we start with you telling us a bit about your business?

John: Sure I am the founder and president of E3 Wealth, a company that provides wealth management services. We are different than most financial services firms in that we work with a range of clients versus seeking to serve only the affluent. Our approach is to use entrepreneurial ways to create more wealth for our clients. We provide services that have integrated wealth management with tax support. It is a change in the industry and a new approach to integrate wealth and tax. Our niche in the overcrowded industry is that we understand the synergy between tax and wealth. We have built our success by focusing on client economy and customization and the psychology of money. Traditional financial services have focused on accumulation of wealth for clients versus utilizing and leveraging wealth for living life.

Cheryl: John, what is your philosophy on being a change leader in your industry?

John: Our focus on purpose, process, and philosophy helps clients think differently about money and finance. We aim to not only change client experiences with wealth management and financial services; we strive to challenge the status quo on how Americans are educated about money. We proactively challenge the current financial models and focus on adding value for our clients through a psychological approach with our clients. People aren't just about the money; they are emotional beings who want to feel understood and cared for.

Cheryl: What has changed in your industry as a result of the shifting demographics, markets, and technologies?

John: Access to information. People can use Google to find information faster than ever before. They have access to information on any financial vehicle and any strategy. Our role is to help our clients make sense of the information in a way that is meaningful and practical for them to use.

(Continued)

Cheryl: As a self-proclaimed change leader, what questions do you ask yourself every day with regard to client service?

John: How do I align with the recommendations and provide value to the client? How can we create more value? Rather than focus on what we can get from the client, we focus on what we can add. We see this as a big opportunity competitively because the financial industry still has many who focus on the "customers should just trust us" versus how can we better understand the customer and earn their trust? A great example is fees: Customers can see behind the curtain but industry has done a poor job of transparency where we add value first prior to charging fees. We have decided as a company of change leaders to show the value for the customer, and then the client decides on compensation. This approach is new and has caused disruption in the industry.

We see the entire industry shifting because clients want transparency and truth. This is different than the majority attitude in the industry of financial advisors which is "Trust me, I am the expert." We have really taken an opposite approach, which is, you don't *have* to trust us until we *prove to you we are trustworthy.*

Cheryl: What do you think needs to change in the industry overall?

John: Everyone needs to have an attitude of lifelong learning and to focus on improving customer relations through adding value. I am a lifelong learner, and our team members are as well, and I believe this is a factor to our success. I attended a three-day intensive seminar at Harvard's Kennedy Executive Center and learned about NLP (Neuro Linguistic Programming) and how to understand people at a deeper level. The course was about behavioral and neuro-economics and how business leaders need to better understand these principles as they impact people's behaviors. Our industry needs to focus on the reality that our clients are emotionally driven.

It is very difficult for people in our industry to understand and deal with shifting from analytical to emotional. However, it is absolutely necessary to transform the industry overall—to lead with emotional awareness and then the analytical.

We need to all challenge the status quo and think differently in how we will deal with people—both our employees and our clients.

Cheryl: What skills do your change leaders in your company need to have in order to drive transformation for your clients and business?

John: We need more change leaders for the next 30 or 40 years, because there will be even more uncertainty and more confusion and we need to provide the emotional support and financial analysis for the U.S. public. That is our vision. Most important, people in our industry have to have an entrepreneurial mind-set, aka "everyone is a leader," to figure out how to add value today. The mind-set needs to be "If I do a good job of adding value we will be compensated." Value first and value creation first. People who work for E3 Wealth, advisor, and staff member—everyone needs to have an entrepreneurial mind-set. Our country was founded on visionaries and change makers.

We do not accept the status quo; we are looking to blaze a new trail. The forefathers that created this country were entrepreneurial and that is the key to our

(Continued)

future success as a company and as a country. In addition to an entrepreneurial attitude, people must develop an abundance mentality, and we educate our team members on this. Abundance is an add-value mind-set. We want people who want to learn—and who are committed to ongoing learning—and who know that we never get there without lifelong learning. There isn't a point where we stop learning.

Cheryl: What is the key to sustaining a culture that is open to continual innovation and change?

John: It starts with senior leadership, my mentor Mark is a model of having the add-value mind-set. He always asks, "If we don't add value then why do it? When we go to conferences and meetings, we are looking to get and learn one thing. We are always looking to learn that "one" thing, and not one of us has the attitude of "been there and done that." If one of us does have the "been there done that" attitude, we have given each other permission to hold ourselves accountable to shifting the mind-set back to being open and flexible and willing to learn.

We focus on all of our people at different levels and different positions to wake up—to become the change champions and to reach the tipping point of transformation and over time. Collectively, you reach a major turning point. In order for our organization to grow and expand and acquire and double production, our business model and our process is all about the people. Mark has an entrepreneurial abundant mind-set. He wants to learn, and he mentors those who show the same desire to learn. Everyone needs to be looking at adding value to co-workers, employees, and customers, which is an abundant mind-set. Mutual respect and understanding about

> the different perspectives is an important approach. We all
> need to focus on the fact that we are focused on the same
> thing—success. We can learn from different perspectives
> and remember we are all moving in the same direction.

John is a great example of a leader who understands that
being a change leader is a mind-set and an approach that can
be taught and learned.

He is also a great example of being a visionary change leader
who wants to transform an industry—the same approach as his
mentor Mark. Later in the book, I will share an interview with
his mentor, Mark, which goes into further depth about the culture and how they establish the systems to remain a change
culture focused on driving transformation.

In support of the theory that great leaders can be made, let's
go back to Whirlpool as an example. Whirlpool has created one
of the most successful leadership development programs within
the corporate arena. Whirlpool's global business success is the
consistent focus on innovation of branded customer solutions.
A major factor attributed to Whirlpool's success is due to the
focus on leadership. CEO Jeff Fettig who has a change-leader
perspective on leadership. In an interview on Whirlpool's success, he was quoted as saying, "Everyone has different definitions
of leadership. For me, leadership is the ability to be a catalyst for
positive change. Each of those words is important. You need to
be a catalyst or a change agent for the company. You need to be
positive and not lead by fear. And change is a constant in any
organization. If you are not changing, you are probably falling
behind. People who take initiative, who strive for positive outcomes for the organization, and who enable and motivate an
organization to change are leaders."

It would be safe to say that Jeff Fettig models being a change leader and the success at Whirlpool is a testament to the leadership he models and the change culture that his leadership has created. In a recent interview he again cites the ability for leaders to be leaders of change: with the U.S. dollar strength—the company will lose a billion dollars in 2015 but *still* have outstanding growth at $19.9 billion. The strategy of Whirlpool leadership was to go for the consumers in the appliance market who would be ready to buy. Prior to the recession of 2008, there were major appliance sales in line with the housing market boom, and now, almost 10 years later, they will be in the market for new appliances in the next year or two. The company had anticipated the possibility of the dollar increasing and had developed plans and approaches to effectively be ahead of this change.

CREATE AN ORGANIZATIONAL CULTURE OF CHANGE LEADERS

The CEO of Whirlpool, Jeff Fettig, is one example of a change leader who has established a culture of change leaders. Another great example is a Latino change leader, Ralph de la Vega who was recently profiled in Delta's Sky Mile magazine on his leadership approach and his big job to be a change leader in the merger of AT&T Mobile and Business Solutions.

He describes a childhood that was filled with change (in my experience many excellent change leaders have overcome many personal childhood and life challenges), coming to the United States as a child and being raised by foster parents while he waited for his parents to be able to live in the United States. Fast forward to 2015 and de la Vega is leading AT&T's efforts to change, transform, and diversify. The big focus under his leadership is to lead AT&T with a futuristic approach. In his division and under his leadership AT&T is thinking big and leading change by focusing consumers and businesses to be aware that they have more wireless needs than ever before. Some of the tools that AT&T uses to create the culture of change is something I mentioned in an earlier chapter, namely The Foundry, which is an innovation hub with an additional hub for change initiatives and innovations taking place at AT&T's Drive Studio in Atlanta. Nationally, AT&T is investing major dollars through the AT&T University to provide the entire work force to go through ongoing and repetitive training and exposure to "being leaders of change." When I worked with AT&T in 2014, I worked with 6,000 of the middle managers as part of an AT&T University Leadership program and my sessions were titled, "Lead with 2020 Vision." The conferences consisted of programming to help the leaders be leaders of change. The Dean of the University, Ken, described the changes that needed to happen with all levels within the company as turning a great big ship in the middle of a couple of icebergs. AT&T is doing all the right things to create a culture of change leaders. The right things include the following five:

1. Providing a compelling vision for the future of AT&T as a fully recognized and top choice for consumers in technology—remember AT&T as a brand was formally known as the monopoly that controlled most of the phone lines in the United States and Canada.
2. Creating the Foundry or Innovation Centers for the specific focus of innovation as an activity. By providing an innovation hub the message to employees and to customers was/is that AT&T was serious about being innovative and being change leaders.

3. AT&T University, providing education and ongoing training on the skills needed to be agile, flexible, and adaptable. The commitment to spend dollars and time on skills development is a key strategy in creating a culture of change leaders.
4. Providing resources and tools to minimize the silo effect and for leaders to make decisions, to lessen bureaucracy, and to increase efficiencies in departments.
5. Staying true and focused to the change-leaders ideal and building performance metrics and rewards on those who are modeling and being change leaders that are driving innovation.

All these points are the components of creating a culture of change leaders. I spoke at a Manufacturing Conference recently and the keynote I delivered was "Leading with 2020 Vision—Build the Workplace of the Future Today" and shared with the group of leaders in manufacturing how the demography and the technology is forcing all leaders to lead the change. The organic and initial reaction is always a sense of wanting to keep things the same while intellectually knowing that to do so is detrimental to the business. I find that leaders *want* to do better and be better and it's the whole chicken-and-the-egg syndrome. What gets priority? Typically the priorities are putting out fires or reacting to everyday challenges rather than spending time building a strategy that is focused on building a company that sets a high standard for innovation and that requires a culture of change leaders. At the conference session, I had one gentleman ask me what a union environment can do with all the realities of the future workplace knowing that unions are structured as hierarchical and traditional entities. My answer?

Unions need to modernize—they need to lead the change that will create a new brand and a new entity that is attractive to younger employees. Right now most young people do not see unions in a positive light. Generation Ys see unions as restrictive; rewards and advancement are based on hierarchy or seniority and not performance; therefore, it's not that appealing an option for them when choosing places to work. Many unions have known this for a long while, and progressive union change leaders are focusing on building a change culture that appeals to the younger generations.

The U.S. Bureau of Labor Statistics reported that union membership fell significantly in 2012, to its lowest level since 1916. Unions have struggled to deal with growing income inequality and to stem the tide of cutbacks in pensions and insurance coverage. The future workplace changes (i.e., workers move from traditional employee status to part-time and contract work and change jobs at a faster pace than ever before) mean the percentage of the workforce open to union organizing and representation will continue to shrink.

The business world has an advantage in that in many ways its functions are much less complex than unions. Typically there is clarity between customers and employees. Union officers have a difficult time versus a leader in a business due to the rules, regulations, and guidelines that must be in place. However, there are progressive unions that are leading the way toward modernization and being models of a change culture. For example, the best employers and worker organizations could do what Kaiser Permanente and their union is doing; they are leading change by building partnerships that nurture employee engagement. Union workers respond well to these partnerships—despite some traditionalist union leaders who argue that all employers can't be trusted. The workers know better. Union workers can tell good supervisors, managers, and employers from bad ones. Unfortunately the structure of unions does not necessarily always create the innovative change culture we are talking about here. Some union leaders remain who are more focused on protecting and reacting to keep things the same rather than looking at ways to partner, grow, and benefit everyone through innovation and change.

A union environment can build a culture of change with some of the following five approaches:

1. Connect and communicate through an open online forum/app where workers can share their thoughts on employers in an industry or region as places to work, and then publish the results widely (kind of like a TripAdvisor platform for unions).

2. Focus on adding value through partnerships with businesses to create win-win and strategic partnerships. This would require union leaders to shift mind-sets to one of future focused versus job protection. As well as a mind-set of positive change.

3. Create talent pools of people within industries/fields and lead change by providing the resources, education, and tools for worker advancement. By creating talent pools, the workers sees the value of staying in the union environment because of increased opportunities to change jobs. A talent pool can be created as an online portal where employers share names of high-performing employees who are ready for advancement when, however, there are no current opportunities within their workplace. The talent pools become online portals for synergistic access to resources (people) that stay within the union environment.

4. Transparency and sustainability to create enhanced branding of unions as a whole. Leading the change of being "unions of integrity" in the way they treat workers globally. Creating recruiting and retention campaigns by focusing on "what's in it for the union member" that goes beyond the current communication of pension and job protection, which are less relevant to younger workers who value learning, growth, and advancement at a higher level than pensions and working in the same job for many years.

5. Last and most important, union leaders need to change the mind-set to consistently add value by providing constant and ongoing training and coaching to the union leaders and the workers. The old style leadership approach of being autocratic or dictatorial does not and will not work with the upcoming generations.

The risk for union leaders who are not change leaders is to continue to focus on keeping and protecting the status quo, which then puts the entire business at risk. A number of unions have closed their doors permanently due to the inability to lead change and transform the culture by partnering with business and to create a modern workplace. The rigidity of sticking to the past and a protective position is the biggest risk to businesses overall. You know the phrase, change or die.

CREATE A CULTURE THAT IS FLEXIBLE, ADAPTABLE, AND ABLE TO CHANGE TO MEET ONGOING MARKET CHANGES

The steps just outlined for creating a culture of change leaders are the organizational steps. How do we go about shifting the mind-set of each person in the company to be more flexible and adaptable? It requires appealing to the individual motivations and unique drivers of each person. In my experience the most time-consuming and yet the most impactful activities when leading change involve spending time with people one-on-one to engage them personally in the calling of the changes that are necessary. Many leaders find that, when they start a change initiative, they start out engaging and enrolling people but then the leaders get caught up again in putting out fires or making other items a greater priority.

The key to successful change leadership and engaging others to be change leaders is to *consistently* invest the time to keep everyone on side. Using project-management tools or calendar tools can ensure that there is a consistent focus. The greater action is for you to make it a priority to be having one-on-ones with all your team members and encouraging your leaders to do the same.

THE DIFFERENCE BETWEEN CHANGE FOR THE SAKE OF CHANGE AND TRANSFORMATIONAL AND SUSTAINABLE CHANGE

There is a difference between change that drives transformation and change for the sake of change. The type of change that is the focus of this book is change that transforms. Creating a culture of change leaders does not mean a constant disruption that takes up time and energy. The context of a culture of transformational change is having individuals who, because they are constantly focused on adding value, recommend changes that are good for the company, teams, and customers.

Change for the sake of change comes from insecurity and fear and a nonabundant mentality. Typically, decisions or ideas generated when someone is in fear are not for the benefit of the overall system. Let's look at a concept mentioned earlier called "restore versus reorganize," as a tool to help identify whether someone is seeking change for the sake of change or if that individual is focused on transformational change.

When a company, business, or individual is focused on "restore" it means they want things to stay the same.

The Merriam-Webster dictionary definition of *restore* is:

> To give back (someone or something that was lost or taken); to return (someone or something); to put or bring (something) back into existence or use; to return (something) to an earlier or original condition by repairing it, cleaning it, etc.

Those who are in "restore" mode will want to create change for the sake of change to preserve their own needs or to protect the status quo. People who are in fear will often want to go back to what is known and what is safe rather than learning and growing to get to the next level.

There are times where restore is a necessary "resting" place after a period of major reorganizational change. When people or companies are in constant and continual restore mode they will:

- Look to stop a change that is transformative and hold back the future.
- See the motivation for restore as fear or loss mentality (I or we are going to lose something).
- Focus on losing something personally and protect status quo.
- Promote CYA and preserve self-identity rather than transform.

- Want to prove it's not their fault and they are not to blame for challenges.
- Be not willing/able to increase energy to the level of learning and growth.

When people are driving transformation, they are in reorganizational mode.

The Merriam-Webster dictionary definition of *reorganizational* is:

> To organize something again or in a different way, to organize again or anew.

Those who are focused on reorganizing are focused as change leaders on change that will create something better than what was before and to transform the status quo. When change leaders are focused on reorganizing, the change is always to make things better, to improve conditions for self and others. Reorganization is an approach that optimizes existing structures while producing new sustainable emerging properties that create growth and evolution, whereas those who are in the restore mode work to keep things the same, even if keeping things the same will be painful. This is not helpful for self or for others. A company that is focused on reorganizing as a constant focus has characteristics such as the following:

- The company and people within the company see disruption or challenges as an opportunity to improve and produce something more efficient and worthwhile.
- Complaints and problems are a gift—an opportunity to learn, grow, and adapt to create better and newer sustainable systems.

- Change leaders utilize creative solutions as reorganizational tools.
- Conflict of any kind is an opportunity to organize at a higher order and to create innovative solutions.
- The questions that are asked are about the overall system and how to make things richer, better, and more sustainable.
- Change leaders and everyone on the team consistently look to add value to others and to the overall system.

A reorganizational approach includes helping others to be change leaders. A master change leader has the energy and the focus to not only consistently reorganize his or her own thoughts and behaviors but also to share energy and resources with others to help them stay focused on being reorganizational.

Here are a few questions for you to think about as they relate to helping others to become change leaders:

- Do you share the philosophy that everyone is a change leader? Why?
- Do you believe change leaders are born, made, or both? Why?
- On a scale of 1–10, with 10 being high, how would you rate yourself on your commitment to being a lifelong leader?
- Do you have an abundant mind-set which means you are focused on "good for all" that constantly looks to add value to others?
- If you are a union leader, are you a change leader that partners with business?
- As a change leader, do you spend a good portion of your time on face-to-face meetings to support the people on your team to be change leaders?

- Are you a leader who is focused on a reorganizational approach? How?
- Do you focus on innovation and creative solutions as a change leader? How?

In this chapter, we looked at how you as a change leader can help others to become change leaders. There is tremendous energy and excitement when staying focused on being a leader who is constantly looking to add value, to reorganize, and to help others succeed and grow as well. A change culture is created by individual energy and contribution, and the best tool is for each of us to model the attributes and behaviors of a transformational change leader. In the next chapter, we will talk about the major impact that technology is having on organizations and individuals, and the opportunities of integrating technological aptitude with valuing people to create transformation.

7

Technology and People—
The Impetus for Change

A leader takes people where they want to go. A great
leader takes people where they don't necessarily want to go,
but ought to be.

—Rosalynn Carter, former First Lady

It is more evident now than ever before that the speed of
technological innovation is creating a massive need to
build businesses that integrate both the opportunities that
technological innovation provides as well as remaining focused
on the impact that fast change has on people (employees and
customers). This quote from a friend and colleague, Dr. Ralph
Kilmann, author of *Quantum Organizations* and *The Courageous
Mosaic*, positions the opportunity of technology and the impact
of change on people beautifully with the following questions:

> What is an organization? What is the role of technology
> in organizations? How fast do technologies change and
> improve? How fast do people change and improve? How
> can organizations make the best use of its technologies
> and people, especially when they change and improve at
> different rates? And how do we resolve the inherent conflict
> between the increasing rate of technological change and
> the increasing difficulty that many people have in adapting
> to that change?

Dr. Kilmann goes on to say that technology is not *new* per se. Rather, he clarifies that technologies have evolved (the key element that is and always will be the same—people) the way that people adapt and come together to achieve more than an individual would on his or her own. Dr. Kilmann continues:

> Regarding technologies: Way back in the Stone Age, humans began creating and using tools (technologies) to overcome their limitations—initially to add to their physical strength, later to communicate beyond the volume/reach of their vocal cords, and ultimately to extend far beyond their information processing and cognitive capacity. Using a boulder example, if one person can use a large stick (a technology) as a crowbar, perhaps he can move the boulder all by himself. But very large boulders can still be too heavy for one person, regardless of the size of the crowbar. To achieve the goal of moving a very large boulder in a particular direction, we need an organization of many people with larger and larger sticks. Subsequently, we can invent huge bulldozers and consciously coordinate people—along with their bulldozers—to move a mountain. Let's define technologies as all the possible extensions that humans create and then use for the purpose of overcoming their limitations—anything from using a crowbar in a stone quarry to using personal data devices to instantly communicate around the globe. Ironically, individuals working alone could never have invented (let alone manufactured and then brought to market) the most complex and sophisticated technologies that we see in the workplace today: Today's technologies (versus yesterday's sticks) could only have been developed by organizations that are consciously coordinating the efforts of many people who are using all sorts of technologies. Recognize this accelerating spiral of human evolution: We use organizations to create new technologies (human extensions), which are then

used by people in other organizations to further overcome their limitations and thus achieve previously unimaginable goals. For example, only a few years back in 2010, who would've thought that scattered citizens sending out tweets on their smartphones could have consciously coordinated the overthrow of a dictatorial regime?

The powerful perspective that Dr. Kilmann provides is that technology innovation is not new; it has been happening since the beginning of human evolution *and* the speed with which new technologies are emerging has been and is accelerating rapidly. So, with this reality, what needs to happen?

TECHNOLOGY IS DRIVING MAJOR CHANGE: WHAT CAN A CHANGE LEADER DO TO EMBRACE IT

In my book, *101 Ways to Make Generations X, Y and Zoomers Happy at Work*, I researched the major impact of generational attitude differences on the future workplace. What I discovered in my research was that the massive changes that were happening were not the result of the generational differences; rather, the changes were due to the impact of the rapid technological changes. It is, in fact, technology that is causing the need for every one of all ages to be able to integrate and leverage technology for the good of both employees and customers. As a change leader, understanding the different aptitudes for both change and for technology can help to better lead others. The goal is to help yourself and others to further embrace technological innovation while increasing the skills of being able to understand and bridge the impact of technology and change on people.

There is a link between the rapid pace of technological improvements in organizations and the pace of improving people's ability to use technologies. Different generations have different types of adaptability to technological change. This is due to the eras in which different technological innovations occurred. For the 1970s, 1980s, and 1990s, only one generational type, the Traditionalists (born before 1946), was dominant in the workplace.

During those decades, there were longer gaps between major technological innovations, and the Traditionalists could more easily adopt the newest technology of their day. Fast-forward to the 1980s and 1990s when the Zoomers (Baby Boomers who refuse to age) and Generation X began entering the workforce and technologies and improvements began accelerating much faster. Today and in the past decade, and more so in the past five years, the newest generation to enter the workforce is Generation Y. This is the generation that has grown up with technology as an inherent part of their upbringing and they are entering the workforce at a time when many organizations are at the crossroads of what is called the digital divide. In my book, *Leadership Mastery in the Digital Age*, I provide a digital fluency quiz (also available on my website www.cherylcran.com/digitalsavvyquiz) that provides a glimpse into the skills aptitude of leaders in the area of digital fluency as well as people leadership ability. The future workplace is a place where change leaders create an environment that is connected, open and sharing and where technology supports the goals and vision while people are the focus.

From a technological adaptation perspective, each generational type grew up with a different set of core technologies and skills and, as a result, acquired a different capacity to readily adopt the next generation of technologies. In order for today's organizations to succeed in these times of accelerating technological change within a highly competitive interconnected global economy, they must learn how to enable all their employees (across all generational types) to learn how to effectively use the latest and greatest extensions (technologies), and to do so at an increasing speed.

What are the opportunities for leaders of change who drive transformation with people and technology?

In this digital age of mobile computing with accelerated interconnectivity across the globe we need to engage everyone (because, remember, everyone is a leader) to be quick and agile adaptors to technology while staying with a primary focus of adding value to people such as employees and customers. You, as a change leader, need to recognize where you can improve your level of leveraging technological tools to increase productivity and innovation. You as a change leader need to eagerly teach yourself to learn and adapt to leverage technology for business *and* you as a change leader must keep an eye open for the ultimate vision, which is to unify the reality of an increasing speed of change with both people and technology.

What can a change leader do to further embrace the impact of technology? Here is a list of ideas and questions to consider:

- Create a newfound awareness and acceptance of the impact of digital fluency in the workplace. For example, do you and your company provide ongoing training and sharing on how to leverage the technological tools that you have available?

- Consider creating a reverse mentoring program in which the innately digitally fluent teach what they know upward and across work units. I have a YouTube video on reverse mentoring here: https://www.youtube.com/watch?v=lR2vspb3VbE.

- Technology and people need to be a part of the strategic focus on engaging employees and customers through technological tools and for leveraging social media for crowdsourcing, surveys, recruiting, and engaging both employees and customers. It's not about whether to use social media; it's about how to leverage it to match your strategic goals.

- There must be commitment to educate all workers on the generational change approaches and values in order to increase understanding and to focus on collaboration and innovation. For example, create forums or leverage the intranet to share and discuss the different approaches to embrace new technologies and to adapt to technological change. Provide strategies on how to leverage the knowledge of each of the generations. For example, a Generation Y may be technologically fluent and adept and yet not have a clear understanding of the business. Or you may have a Zoomer who has in-depth business experience and yet refuses to learn the new technology that has been introduced. Or you could have a Generation X who has both the technology skill and the business skill and yet doesn't want to share his or her knowledge with anyone because he or she wants to protect (restore) his or her role or job. The opportunity with all of the described scenarios is to create a culture to share knowledge via job shadow and video tutorials, by providing training, and by incentivizing the sharing of resources.

LEAD CHANGE IN A MULTIPLE DEVICES REALITY

Information technology and business are becoming inextricably interwoven. I don't think anybody can talk meaningfully about one without talking about the other.

—Bill Gates

We are faced with the reality that we are living and working in a technological reality that impacts every area of our lives. The change that has been created because of the innovations in technology such as smartphones and multiple devices cannot be ignored. As leaders of change, there is an imperative for everyone to adapt with speed and agility to the pace of technological change.

A recent Google study says that 90 percent of people move between devices to accomplish a goal whether that's on smartphones, laptops, tablets, or TV. We have become a nation of multiscreen users. Smartphones are the preferred devices for those on the go, as well as for those at home to communicate and connect, to access information quickly and immediately and in short bursts of time. The same survey states that 38 percent of our daily interactions occur on a smartphone. Fifty-four percent of smartphone activity is motivated by communication and 33 percent by entertainment. Smartphones are the most common starting point for online activities. Quick searching and data lookup start on the smartphone and from there 60 percent move to a laptop to continue their online activity. Sixty-three percent use their smartphone for online shopping and 66 percent use it for social networking.

The Google research also found that nine out of 10 people use multiple screens sequentially, and that smartphones are by far the most common starting point for sequential activity. So completing a task like booking a flight online or managing personal finances doesn't just happen in one sitting on one device. In fact, 98 percent of sequential screeners move between devices in the same day to complete a task. There is a user personality type that is more geared toward multiple-devices use; however, the trends are going to continue for more and more people as per the Google research. In my opinion, the multiple-device user is someone who is a driver personality who wants to get things done now and who wants to get results quickly. I move between multiple devices constantly, and I believe it's partly because I am an entrepreneur. I use my smartphone and the apps on it for quick access to information, for texting, and for social media. When I have project work to do, I am on my MacBook Air, and when I want to feel as if I am not working I use my iPad Air. Having multiple devices gives me the freedom to access information on multiple platforms. For example, in my business, I need to have quick access to my speaking calendar. I have the app on my iPhone and iPad so that I can quickly check there, and if I am on my laptop, I can go to the web to get the schedule. Teenagers and those in their 20s have been innately moving between multiple devices (gaming consoles/PDAs/laptops) throughout most of their lives, whereas Traditionalists and some Zoomers are less likely to move through multiple devices in the way they use technology in life or work.

SO WHAT ARE THE IMPLICATIONS IN THE WORKPLACE?

Your attitude and positioning about multiple devices and social media will determine whether this reality causes you to want to restore back to the good old days or whether you are in full-on reorganizational mode, which is to embrace and leverage what technology can do. If you view social media and multiple devices as the reality of today's technology and you see it as an opportunity to leverage productivity, social media sharing, and innovation, then you will approach this from an open leadership and reorganizational attitude. If you view social media and multiple devices as frustrating, difficult to manage, and unproductive, then you will approach this from a limited (restore) perspective and from a closed leadership attitude.

Right now, as I write this chapter, I have used my iPhone 6 to respond to a text, to post a note to Facebook, and to make a quick note to follow up on an item in my Evernote app and make a credit card payment on my Square app. I am on my MacBook Air with Word, Firefox, Safari, Skype, and my e-mail open. I am moving between writing, researching online, responding to IM's through Skype and my e-mail. You might be thinking that I am probably unfocused, stressed, and unproductive, and yet I am focused, relaxed, and getting a lot done in this writing day. I have adapted to managing multiple sources of information and input while working in a multitasking and multiple-device reality. This can cause one either stress or an adaptive response. Increased popularity and developments in communication through technology has pushed individuals to constantly multitask on their wireless devices.

An example is the e-learning environment in which students are constantly working on assignments while watching online lectures, taking notes, and referencing information online. Everyone is influenced by the immediate interaction that exists between individuals and information in today's rich media environment. The ability to have immediate access provides an incentive and opportunity to individuals to upgrade the operating system to be able to run multiple streams of thought and access information. As I mentioned earlier, on upgrading the leadership operating system, the technological impact requires us to expand our minds to include multiple activities, multiple perspectives, and, of course, multiple devices. Task management has changed; it used to be focused and done in a one-at-a-time manner, but now, with technology, the tasks are often unstructured and unknown. The internal competing mind factors are attention and memory.

When a task requires multiple cognitive processes, one task will be faded out. Newer research has found that users "killed less time" while multitasking and accomplish what they are working on when using multiple programs and/or multiple devices. Specifically, in the classroom environment, the use of multiple devices can help further exploration of the information that is being covered in class while it is being presented.

When I present to audiences, I often joke that, although I am talking, people are likely texting, checking out the weather, or Web surfing! All joking aside, more and more people are looking up content while they are listening to a speaker, or in my case they are interacting with me or tweeting out sound bites which I have asked them to do.

Research from Dell Global Evolving Workforce Study Trend identified a few key trends regarding multiple devices. One of them is that one size doesn't fit all, and the report confirms that wherever and whenever they are working, employees are using multiple devices, rather than just one to get their jobs done. Eighty-one percent of those surveyed said that their top priority in a device was performance.

Location of work also has an impact on the devices used. Sixty-two percent of employees consider the desktop computer as their primary business device while at work, with the highest use in financial services, public healthcare, and government, but when doing work at home, laptops are used as frequently as desktops. For personal purposes, employees are switching to more mobile forms of technology when laptop, tablet, and 2-in-1 usages are higher than when working in the office. Fifty-one percent of employees use IM or e-mail colleagues as a productivity tool when people are located physically near them, rather than talking with them directly. Globally, more than half of employees currently use personal devices for work purposes and are secretly using personal devices for work without the company knowing, with smartphones and laptops being those most frequently used.

CHANGE LEADERS LISTEN UP—THE SECRET TO HAPPY EMPLOYEES? TECHNOLOGY

One out of four employees globally report they are influenced by the technology provided to them at work and would consider taking a new position if provided better technology that helps them be more productive. Employees in the media and entertainment sector are most likely to quit over poor technology. Those in management roles and employees in emerging markets, in particular, expect the best technology in order to stay with their current employer or they would consider a new employer. Seventy-six percent of employees said technology has had an influence on the way they worked in the past year. Forty-six percent said technology has increased their productivity and enabled them to communicate faster.

As a leader of change, you must be adaptable to workers who are not agile multitaskers and those who are. In certain job functions multitasking is an asset, whereas in others it may be more of a hindrance.

Ask yourself the following four questions as they relate to multiple devices in the workplace and multitasking:

1. Who on your team is good at multitasking with multiple devices? What makes them good at it?
2. What functions and tasks in your department require focus and less reliance on multitasking and multiple devices?
3. What is your company policy on BYOD (bring your own device)? Does it make your IT team crazy or has IT come up with solutions to make it workable?
4. What do you think is the happy medium between multi-tasking and direct focus?

When I present to audiences, I recognize that the majority of the audience is on either their smartphones or their tablets. Rather than fight this reality, I openly encourage everyone to leave their phones/devices on and I encourage them to tweet, and use Facebook, Instagram, and more while I am presenting. I also get them to text me while I present because this helps audience members ask questions that they do not want to ask out loud. I believe this is the new reality and I have integrated it rather than insist that everyone turn off his or her devices. I don't see it as disrespectful if someone is on their device while I am presenting; I see it as an audience member taking notes, tweeting, or texting. In fact, when I am in an audience, I have my devices on and with me and I am taking notes, checking e-mail, and looking up URLs that are mentioned in the presentation. Often, I get magnificent ideas from a presentation and I want to tweet insights, ideas, and information to my circles.

Dick Escue, CIO at RehabCare Inc., a St. Louis–based provider of postacute healthcare services, has a leg up on many of his peers when it comes to mobile device management (MDM).

He foresaw the infiltration of personal mobile devices into the workplace four years ago. When his tech services team warned him in 2007 that the company's BlackBerry-carrying management would be clamoring for iPhones, and told him IT had better nip those requests in the bud, he did what a change leader would do and focused on the opportunity to be ahead of the changes he foresaw. He instructed his department to figure out a way to say yes.

"We embraced the iPhone, gave it to the people who wanted it, and they were thrilled," Escue recalled. "And they loved us as a result of it."

Since then, step-by-step, Escue has made the Apple iOS integral to RehabCare's computing environment—and, in his view, a competitive business advantage. His IT team has equipped thousands of field therapists with iPhones and iPads to mobilize mission-critical processes, from a preadmission hospital screening app built on the Force.com platform to a caregiver app developed with healthcare vendor Casamba Inc. The iPad is the business-meeting tool of choice for RehabCare executives, and is fast becoming the workstation for RehabCare's clinical staff.

As for the demarcation between personal and corporate devices, Escue suspected that employees would take better care of their devices if they regarded them as their own. If iPhone and iPad users need help connecting their personal iTunes accounts, IT tells them how to do it. This is a great example of providing added value, recognizing that the employee will appreciate being able to have personal-use questions answered in addition to work-related questions with their devices. Escue's deployment of an all-Apple workplace is the poster child for a CIO's embrace of customer service in IT. Operating in this way, however, is becoming the norm rather than the exception for IT departments, with enterprises' uptake of mobile devices.

As many organizations work to integrate BYOD into the workplace the other technology being given much attention is social media in the workplace.

LEAD CHANGE IN A SOCIAL MEDIA REALITY

Whether your organization has a social media positive approach or a social media ambivalent approach, we cannot ignore its proliferation of use among all demographics. Social media in business is no longer just the domain of marketing. The use of social media technologies—from Twitter-like activity streams to sharing sites with a Facebook feel—is being promoted, packaged, and *used inside* companies. Building the social workplace is about being social, and being social for the greater good of the business, in increased worker productivity and greater innovation. Sites like Yammer (https://www.yammer.com) provide internal social media for organizations.

Social media has the potential to improve the ability of the corporate workforce, from the senior management to the front line, to engage in meaningful and real-time communication and collaboration. Advocates of workplace social media argue that the tools help uncover the knowledge that exists within a company by moving away from traditional organizational hierarchies and minimizing silos or departmental boundaries. Tools like wikis and blogs, for example, allow executives to see what employees view as valuable to the company and allow employees to voice their concerns. In turn, employees get a better sense of what is valuable to a company in terms of its corporate goals and values.

Social media can spur innovation—whether, through the sharing of ideas, or, simply by communicating. One example involved an employee at Lowe's Companies Inc. who asked via the company's social network how to get more inventory of a particular paint tray. When a fellow employee on the network asked how this person had sold out of inventory, she explained that a video demo she had made for using the paint tray had tripled its sales. The demo was scaled companywide, resulting in millions of dollars in additional sales.

The Mayo Clinic is an advocate of social media and its role in medicine. They were early adopters of podcasts, YouTube, Facebook, and Twitter and have created their own internal Center for Social Media just two years ago. Questions about privacy and information sharing via social media are just some of the frequently asked questions of the Mayo Clinic's social media programs. The medical director Dr. Timimi says that they guide their employees to think carefully about what they post. They also stress that the tools are for professional medical education and engagement. Many workplaces have blocked access to Facebook and Twitter because they are worried about productivity. The Mayo Clinic took a different approach and, in fact, studies show communicating via social media about work can allow employees to bypass restrictions of time zones or geography, boosting productivity by as much as 25 percent. Leading teams in multiple devices and social media reality is causing leaders to adapt quickly to the impact that technology is making on the workplace. In addition, it is forcing leaders to look at the positives as they relate to increased productivity, personal buy-in, and greater innovation.

Some final tips on leading change with technology and people:

- Assess your current level of technological adaptability; is there an opportunity for you to increase your technology skills?
- Who could you learn from? Do you have a Generation Y on the team who is a tech whiz and who you could spend time with weekly on upgrading your tech skills?

- Does your IT department support your employees as customers and provide superior tech support, and are they leading the change with BYOD?
- Does your company use social media portals within the company such as Yammer? Or do you allow the use of Facebook?
- Do you provide regular training on professional social media etiquette by providing the dos of good social media usage and examples of when it has been done right?
- Do you have a flexible mind-set as it relates to multitasking and multiple devices?
- If you do have a social-media-friendly approach or you use an internal social-media tool such as Yammer, are you maximizing the collaboration potential? Is everyone using the technology, and if not how can you increase engagement?

As Dr. Ralph Kilmann stated in his overview of how technologies have evolved from the beginning of mankind to where they are today, technology has always been a part of human reality *and now* we are faced with the opportunity of leveraging technology by focusing on *people*.

WHERE TECHNOLOGY AND PEOPLE CONVERGE—THE FOCUS NEEDS TO BE ON PEOPLE WHILE INTEGRATING TECHNOLOGY

The art of change leadership requires that, as change leaders, you are able to integrate both a tech-savvy approach along with a people-savvy approach.

Table 7.1   The Difference between Tech-Savvy Skills and
            People-Savvy Skills

Tech-Savvy Change Skills	People-Savvy Change Skills
Easily adapts to technology. Able to leverage technology to increase business results. Able to quickly learn and adapt to changes in technology. Able to increase efficiencies and speed of tasks for self and others through technology.	Easily adapts to people and personalities/generations/cultures. Able to leverage results by honoring, respecting, and coaching people. Able to quickly learn and adapt to people's behaviors and attitudes.

For the purpose of understanding the distinction between a change leader's tech-savvy skills and people-savvy skills, check out Table 7.1.

The technological revolution has caused many leaders to focus more on the technological aspects of the work, and many leaders have lost sight of good change-leadership tactics, need a reminder about them, or have never been exposed to them.

As you can see from Table 7.1, being solely tech savvy would be a one-dimensional approach to change leadership. A leader that is tech-savvy would have the skills to leverage technology but not the skills to inspire, coach, and influence people. A change leader who is only people-savvy would have great relationships based on people skills, but would not have the leadership ability nor the respect of teams. The overall goal is to integrate both the tech-savvy skills with the people-savvy skills to be a change leader who can transform business in a fast-paced world.

8

Tools for Transformation

An integral approach acknowledges that all views have a degree of truth, but some views are more true than others, more evolved, more developed, more adequate.

—Ken Wilber

Transformation is not a solitary activity. Well it is and it isn't. I know I am contradicting myself here—first, each individual goes through his or her transformative process. Then there is a sense of an obligation or a drive to want to share the transformation process with others, and from there is a collective movement toward overall transformation of a system, a process, a culture, a company, a government, and so on.

I have covered a lot in this book about transformation of self, of thoughts, and of the need for upgrading the leadership/ human operating system. In order to truly drive transformation the focus ultimately needs to be on a "we" approach that is grounded in a deep and abiding desire to create a new organizing principle or system that supports the transformation we seek to achieve. The process of transformation is not solely of the mind; it is of the energy reality that we wish to create. This book is an evolutionary approach to change and transformation, and the evolutionary approach is that we as individuals are constantly evolving and elevating our understandings and our structures and our behaviors in order to create higher and more effective orders of how we do things. Evolutionary change leadership is focused on creating change that "frees up more energy" for self and others. When we free up more energy we are able to more easily add value, which is the biggest success component of change leadership mentioned earlier in this book.

Shifting the context of change and transformation from purely a "we have to get everyone on board so we can make more profit or have more business" toward a "we want to shift the entire culture of the organization toward everyone being focused on adding value and therefore adding energy to the system."

We often think of energy as something we consume to heat our homes or fuel our cars. Here in this book in the context of change and transformation there is another way to look at energy: in that there is a tremendous amount of available energy that can be harnessed by humans through the ability to connect to the field of energy that exists all around us and choosing to create more energy through conscious awareness of thought, words, and actions. When you think of any charismatic person, the defining component of what makes that person charismatic is what? Energy. He or she exudes a vibrant energy that attracts us to him or her.

I have had the distinct privilege of deepening my understanding of energy and its impact on individuals, workplaces and business through a variety of master teachers. One theory that I have been a student of is Integral Theory by Ken Wilber. Wilber is a renaissance man in that he is at the forefront of creating the AQAL Model that is being used in businesses as a tool to bring awareness and to help drive transformation to an "energy" approach to business. The AQAL model was created by examining all of the cultural models on human potential, social growth, spiritual growth, and psychological growth and putting them all together to create an integral model.

The AQAL map/model distills all research on human potential into five key elements for the purpose of evolution of individuals and cultures. The five elements are quadrants, levels, lines, states, and types and they are not theoretical—they are actual experiences of the human reality.

The use of this map is applicable to many aspects of living and very applicable to business and everyday living. With a map you have an extensive resource available to refer to and to help identify the direction you need to go and to map out where you want to be.

On the journey toward self-transformation the AQAL map is a tool to build awareness and to use the principles to vastly and rapidly increase your personal evolution. As we move the others and the collective toward transformation the AQAL map is an accountability tool, a reference tool, and a brand new way of building cultures, strategies, and ways to add value for both employees and clients. It is an ultimate tool to drive transformation.

The AQAL map is also known as the Integral Operating System and is one of the "how to" systems to upgrade the human operating system.

The five elements as mentioned are the key components to being able to read the map, bring the map into your awareness, and to utilize the understandings to increase your ability to drive transformation for yourself and others.

States of consciousness are a key part of the AQAL map: the states of dreaming and waking, which are widely known, but states of consciousness also include meditative states, altered states, and peak experiences.

The Integral Operating System process is to consciously be aware of the states of consciousness and to choose to elevate awareness and insights that come from each state.

States of consciousness are transitory; they change and can do so in a moment whereas the *levels* of consciousness do not. The stages identify levels and development; they represent the milestones of growth. Once you master a level of development you have continual ability to access the knowing from that stage. Think of it like a tennis player; once you have mastered the backhand you can always use it as a tool when playing the game of tennis. If you never master the backhand you may be relegated to always using the same forehand play, which would greatly diminish your ability to play the game fully.

The AQAL model has eight to 10 levels of consciousness development—here I will share three of the stages for the purpose of you having a sense of the power of the model as a transformation tool.

The three components that I will share are egocentric, ethnocentric, and worldcentric, which are directly related to the concept of "change is a we" approach.

The egocentric is the moral development of a sense of an "I" whereas ethnocentric is a shift to the "us" and worldcentric is a shift of awareness to include the entire world. These three AQAL map components could also be seen as body, mind, and spirit. Egocentric is a focus on the physical reality where you are most identified with the "me" reality, the ethnocentric is the mind which begins to see correlations between shared values or common interests, and the spirit is worldcentric where you see all things common to all human beings.

So this brief overview of the AQAL map provides a resource or a tool to deepen your discovery of transformation tools that are available.

WHAT TYPE OF TRANSFORMER ARE YOU?

Given the three elements shared above of egocentric, ethnocentric, and worldcentric I am sure you can feel the energetic pull of wanting to develop your ability to be worldcentric. Remember that as we develop levels and states of development we always have that development available as a resource.

For the following statements answer yes or no—there are no "maybe" or "sometimes" answers. Simply go with a straightforward yes or no gut response to the questions.

1. I have a strong sense of self, I know who I am, I know what I want, and I know what I am capable of.
___Yes ___No

2. I have a strong sense of a mission, a purpose, and what I am supposed to be doing in my work. ___Yes ___No

3. I have a calling. I feel drawn to create transformation for others. ___Yes ___No

4. I find it easy to find common ground with others, to find similarities. ___Yes ___No

5. I find it easy to enjoy others' individualism and differences from me. ___Yes ___No

6. I am able to easily link my understandings of things to others' understandings to create common understandings. ___Yes ___No

7. I am able to see the world vision. I easily relate what I do and what others do to the overall bigger impact on the world. ___Yes ___No

8. I am focused on making the world a better place; I look at the impact I make in my work and in my life as an impact on the world. ___Yes ___No

9. I am driven/called to be part of something bigger than myself, some cause, some bigger impact actions.
___Yes ___No

10. I easily inspire others to come on the journey with me. I bring immense energy to others by providing resources, support, and encouragement ___Yes ___No

For an online version of this quiz and for more options go to www.cherylcran.com/worldcentricleader.

If you answered yes to most of the questions, you are a worldcentric transformer, you are focused on the big picture, you want to make big impacts for the benefit of the entire ecosystem. You care about the impact that you make as a leader on the bigger system and you are concerned about making the world a better place through your work and your contributions, and you motivate and inspire others to come join you on the journey to make a joyful contribution to the world.

If you answered yes to questions one to six you are ethnocentric with a deep understanding of yourself in relation to others. You have a healthy egocentric understanding and you are expanding your awareness toward more of a "we" approach versus a "me" approach. Your opportunity is to stretch and reach for the worldcentric approach which will not only fuel you as a transformer and give you more personal energy it will also bring massive energy to your "tribe" or your teams as you evolve and bring along others on the transformational path.

If you answered yes to questions one to three and no to the rest of the questions, you are spending time in the egocentric realm and your opportunities are to increase your reach to include others in your transformation journey. As a transformer when you make the stretch from "me" to "we" you infuse more trust, more sharing, and more engagement from all of those around you.

Everyone is a transformer; everyone is on the path to transformation. The awareness of where you are on the transformation journey allows for you to become aware, to acknowledge where you are and to accept where you are and then to consciously choose to go up the ladder, if you will, to the next level. The art of change leadership is the humble appreciation that no matter how masterful we may become at any given task, role, or project we are always humble students. True transformers recognize that they have never arrived; they recognize that the true reward is in the learning, in the awakenings, in the journey toward higher and higher levels of mastery.

Life and work has a way of bringing us to reality when we come from a place of arrogance or "been there done that." I don't know about you but I have had and will continue to have many wake-up calls in order to keep me a humble student on her journey toward mastery as a leader of change.

I have had many wonderful bosses in my career and when I look back I have been blessed with some very honest and caring bosses who had the courage to give very valuable and honest feedback to me. Back in the early nineties I worked for a national mortgage insurance company as an area manager. I was young, in my late twenties and I had been head hunted away from a major bank to work for the mortgage insurance company. My ego was pretty inflated with the fact that I had been wooed away from a high-paying job in banking to come and work for this smaller, private, and growing company. When I showed up for my first month on the job I was super inflated with my past successes and approached my team form the egocentric perspective that I was a superstar. I proudly shared my accomplishments and was quick to point out when I had created a success for the team. I was the leader of a team of sales/broker associates and I was hard pushing with them to reach our targets and goals. One day my boss, Donna called me in to have a chat at the end of the day. No one else was in the office and she was very casual, calm, and relaxed with me. Donna was a fantastic model of an ethnocentric leader although I did not know that at the time. The first thing she asked me was, "Cheryl, you have been here a month; how do you feel like it's been going?"

Immediately I saw this as an opportunity to brag about my accomplishments and I began to regale her with the many tales and examples of how wonderful I was and the results I was creating. Donna listened, she smiled, she nodded her head and then she said, "So how is your team doing?" I still didn't get it and I continued to talk about how I as their leader was creating fantastic results. Then she said, "You know Cheryl I have heard you for the last 20 minutes tell me how wonderful you are and that's great *and* there is something of really high value to be learned in being quietly confident." Silence. Donna sat there and looked at me with the most compassionate smile as I sat there and absorbed what she had said. I felt the power of what she had just said, I paused, I took it in and I got very teary-eyed. I had nothing else to say. Donna went on to say, "You know, Cheryl, it is clearly evident to everyone that you are highly talented and highly capable *and* your next opportunity is to help *others* be talented and wonderful: *pass it on.* That is what a great leader does and I know you have the makings of a great leader."

That day was a transformative day for me, Donna showed me the opportunity for me to shift up a level, to go from being ego-centric to being ethnocentric and she did it in a way that was honoring to who I was while holding an ideal for me to strive toward. Donna was truly a change leader who drove transformation. Her ethnocentric approach has always stayed with me and she continued to be an amazing transformational coach and mentor to me while I remained with that company.

I credit Donna with helping me accelerate my career and more importantly with helping me to become completely committed to the journey of being a master change leader and to contributing to where I am today.

Take a few moments and think about the leaders you have had in your career who were/are able to help you to transform.

What were/are the traits that he or she had, what did you learn, and how have you integrated that learning into who you are as a change leader today?

The traits of an ethnocentric and worldcentric transformational leader are:

- Has healthy self-identity and ego *and* has awareness to know when he or she is being self-focused or self-serving
- Has a keen desire to learn and grow and remains a humble student
- Is open to feedback, honest assessment, and incorporates the feedback right away into his or her life and work
- Has the ability to bring tremendous compassion to others and provides feedback in a way that builds the other person up and makes him or her want to elevate, get better, and be better
- Inspires and engages others by modeling the actions and behaviors of someone who is focused on others' well being and added value
- What else?

As I write this chapter, I am infused with tremendous amounts of energy. On each leg of the transformation journey I continue to be "turned on" by the constant learning and growth. There is so much to learn! It never ends!

RECOGNIZE AND ADAPT TO THE TYPES OF TRANSFORMERS AROUND YOU

The great thing about heightened levels of awareness around self is that you build a hyper vigilant awareness that helps you to recognize similar behaviors when you come across them in others.

In my experience once I have learned a specific lesson or have been through a challenge that created deeper knowledge and insight my ability to see the patterns of behavior in others increases. So, for example, the story I shared with you earlier in the chapter about my being egocentric and my boss Donna guiding me toward ethnocentric was one way that I learned how to see others' behaviors when they were being egocentric.

So how do you recognize the types of transformers around you?

You begin to use the lens of "we" to assess where you yourself are and where others are. The AQAL model has many other levels as mentioned and I do encourage you to discover and immerse yourself in a deeper understanding of it overall. If we use the simple three levels as shared here you can begin to keep an eye out for noticing where people are. You will notice when others are being egocentric because his or her focus is on:

- What he or she is doing right and well
- What he or she is doing to contribute to the team
- What he or she is doing better than everyone else
- What he or she is superior at
- Mostly focused on self

You will notice when others are being ethnocentric because his or her focus will be on:

- What he or she is doing *with* others
- What he or she is doing to *help* others
- What he or she is doing to create more energy for others
- What he or she is enjoying about the differences of others
- What he or she is learning from others

You will notice when others are being worldcentric because his or her focus will be on:

- What he or she wants to see for the world overall through self and others
- What he or she wants the company to do to contribute to the world
- What he or she wants to help others do to help contribute to the world
- What he or she does to inspire and engage others on the mission/vision to make the team/company/world a better place

When someone is egocentric, coach and guide them with compassionate awareness, ask them guiding questions, seed ideas on how he or she can grow and learn and inspire from an ethnocentric level. When someone is ethnocentric, support, praise, and encourage that level and stretch them up to the worldcentric opportunity where there is even more energy and potential to create positive transformation for self and others. When someone is worldcentric, encourage them to share their understanding, to expand their creative ideas, and to coach/guide others to become worldcentric transformers.

DRIVING TRANSFORMATION AS A TEAM OF CHANGE LEADERS

I have mentioned energy a few times in this book and you have likely intuited by now that I am a big believer in the transformational power of "energy management" as it relates to human potential. I have also mentioned that I have been a student of Dr. Epstein's work on energy states and how it relates to transformation.

One of his many tools is something he calls the energy states. The energy states are another model that when deeply understood can shift the paradigm of how you look at transformation. I know for me it added a layer of depth and of greater access to help others transform. In my work I use the energy states as a continual resource and, as an approved licensee of Epstein Technologies Corporate Program, I share the energy states content in my keynotes and trainings. For more information you can go to www.cherylcran.com/epsteintechnologies.

I wish to share with you here an overview of the energy states as it relates to transformation as an additional tool for your toolkit as a transformer.

Dr. Epstein says that it's not time we are looking to harness in today's fast-changing reality, rather it is energy. We all have the same amount of time in each day and why is it that some can achieve amazing outcomes in one day and another cannot? The answer is quite simply, *energy*.

Energy is readily available around us and many do not know how to harness it or access it as a resource. The energy states are: energy poor, energy neutral (low and high), and energy rich.

The ability to understand the impact of energy as a resource and to be able to utilize it as a resource is *the* future of the workplace. Human psychology is such that most people are creatures of habit and also most people repeat patterns even if those patterns do not add value or energy. The insights provided by Dr. Epstein help us to become aware, to acknowledge, and accept the reality of the impact of energy on how we interact with, engage, and affect others.

In Dr. Epstein's words, "The source of power that makes progress possible is energy."

The energy state is the baseline of where a company is overall or where an individual is; the energy required to make a change requires a higher baseline.

Let's take a look at the energy states and the meanings of them as they relate to being a transformer that drives change.

The first energy state is energy poor. This state happens when an event occurs that takes you from manageable to a crash. For example your company loses a major client, your industry suffers a catastrophe, your competitor steals your top talent, or your business partner steals money from the business. When a business or an individual is in an energy-poor state, the experience is that things are not working anymore, there is a disruption, nothing you can do can change it and it's time to bail.

When a company is in energy-poor state, the overall energy of the company is of being in survival mode. Behaviors include sadness, apathy, foreboding, and listlessness; there literally is not enough energy. The behaviors of people within an energy-poor business include autocracy, lack of trust, controlling people and ideas, ignoring client and customer value, and holding on to power.

The highest goals when a company or individual is in an energy-poor state are to survive a little longer and to protect. Any change made from an energy-poor state results in not enough energy. There is not even enough energy to be open to creative solutions. Think of yourself for a moment and remember a time when you have been energy-poor—lacking vision, without enough energy to create, and apathetic about positive change. Organizations that are energy-poor find themselves missing competitive opportunities. Think of Kodak, as mentioned earlier in the book; the age of digital came upon them and rather than reorganize to a higher level of energy and being leaders of the change, the overall energy-poor response was apathy.

There is not a company or an individual who can afford being in a consistently energy-poor state. In this fast-paced reality, the speed of change requires a higher level of energy, which brings us to the next energy state, namely energy-neutral.

Energy neutral is where many companies and individuals hang out. Let's face it, there is an appropriate time for each of the energy states to shift. We will all experience energy-poor states as a result of a sudden change *and* it is the speed with which we recognize the signs of the states and then use strategies to consciously elevate the states to the highest energy level possible that helps us transform and help others transform at a more rapid pace. As a tool for transformation, developing the ability to recognize energy states and to take action to rise to higher energy state levels is a key strategy to upgrade the leadership operating system. In addition, it is a tool that can be applied when interacting with others, coaching others, strategizing the business, and even in managing our personal lives. Energy neutral has a range—from low energy neutral to high energy neutral.

Let me explain, energy neutral on its own means it's like being in neutral in a car. The car stays where it is, the engine is revving, there is enough energy to keep the car running but without putting more energy, that is, gas and pedal to the metal, the car stays idle.

There are times throughout the day for a company when energy neutral is the place to be and when we would spend a good portion of our time. For example writing e-mails, writing a book, and doing repetitive tasks are all energy-neutral tasks. Companies go through energy-neutral cycles when they are either upgrading from an energy-poor state to energy rich, and then they need to make things happen by creating energy richness and then spend time in higher energy neutral when implementing the energy-rich vision.

We could add energy rich (more on that later) to our energy-neutral tasks, which would increase energy and productivity. Energy neutral can be a major trap, a state in which companies and individuals convince themselves that good is good enough. Companies may justify the level of success they have achieved and desire no more. Individuals may be comfortable but not stretch to achieve their heart's desire. There may be a prevalent cultural belief that effort is a substitute for progress with attitudes of, "if it's hard it must be working," rather than, a culture of thinking, "if we raise the energy state things will organize at a higher level and there will be more synergy and more ease of progress." Many companies are in an energy-neutral pattern because of cultural business-operation patterns based on history or time in business or how things have been done repeatedly, rather than on challenging the status quo and bringing more energy into the system to create higher energy.

In lower energy neutral there are stories, excuses, justifications, and a myriad of reasons that something cannot or will not work. It is low energy neutral because the energy is focused on why something cannot happen rather than on bringing more energy that says, "here's how we can do it."

When a company or individual is in low energy neutral, it's like the car is in neutral and the engine is losing gas and sputtering or idling rough. In lower energy neutral, companies will experience no discernible progress and will have excuses for why there is no progress. Lower energy neutral companies and people engage in the blame game, in which there are finger pointing, excuses, and rationalizations.

Higher energy neutral on the other hand is about optimizing and is higher functioning. High energy neutral consists of creative solutions, of seeing the opportunity in a loss or change, in taking positive action and getting things done. However, even high energy neutral can be a trap in that a company can be lulled into accepting that good is good enough, with no desire to increase energy to a more consistent energy-rich focus.

Today, energy neutral is the norm for most of culture, overall. The range within energy neutral from low to high is where the majority of the population resides. The energy state of high energy neutral is where progress happens and there is more available energy for the company, employees, and clients. The focus for companies and change leaders needs to be on *valuing energy richness and high energy neutral* as the dominant energy states.

The CEO and the executive of the organization *must* be energy-rich at least 50 percent of the time in their interactions in order to create an energy state that permeates the culture and sets the energetic tone.

When focusing on high energy neutral and into energy-rich (more on that in a bit) the lens through which companies and leaders need to look includes the following perspectives: have a hunger for greatness; have a compelling vision for the future; leverage what is successful already to future success; and focus on breakthrough ideas, innovation, and creative solutions.

The ultimate quest to create available energy for self and others leads us to the most resourceful state of all three states, which is energy-rich.

Energy rich in a company is exhibited when there is so much energy created by a company as a brand that success is ongoing, there is a synergy among the people working in the company, and there is a constant focus on adding high value to all; the people within the company are consistently spending time in energy-rich states such as optimism, creativity, innovation, and worldcentric focus. People within an energy-rich company have developed tools and strategies to help them stay focused on future and solution. Energy-rich company leaders also hold themselves and people accountable and call out excuses or blame for self and for others in order to continue raising the energy state of the company and for the people within the company.

Energy-rich companies and leaders are about future and progress. An unexpected event could happen and the automatic response would be to turn it into a win or a gain for the company. Two good questions to determine if your company or you are operating at an energy-rich level are:

1. Are we experiencing effortless progress?
2. Is progress happening synergistically and with ease?

If your answer is yes to both these questions, then you know that your company and you are spending the majority of your time in energy-rich states. As a change leader who is driving transformation, here are more energy-rich questions to ask about you yourself:

How can I be excellent?
How can I master this?
How can I make this happen?
What can we do to be the *best* company in our industry?

Using the energy states as a tool of transformation, you might be asking, how? Well, the first step is to educate and bring awareness of energy as a resource to the entire company. Energy management is a newfound way of creating results and of being. The workforce has been socially and societally ingrained to believe that time is limited and that working hard is the only way to progress. With energy mastery leaders, teams and companies begin to enjoy the work more, to work toward a common vision and purpose and synergistically create an add-value approach to employees and clients. The time is right for the awareness and the leverage of energy as a resource. Companies are struggling with managing massive amounts of information and individuals are seeking wisdom to leverage the information. When we talk about driving transformation in a fast-paced world, we need new ideas and new ways to be able to thrive in this new modern information age.

You might be thinking that it is not realistic for any company or person to be in an energy-rich state consistently. Similar to the AQAL model of Ken Wilber, once you have learned a level—and in this case you learn how to access and stay energy rich—you always have it as a resource.

Once you have built awareness around energy rich as a resource through education, training, and application, you now use that awareness to create new structures. One way of doing this is for a company to reevaluate its processes, its policies, and procedures. In my work as a consultant, I have found that many organizations are still adhering to policies that were established a decade ago, and those policies are energy-poor to energy neutral as they relate to adding value to employees and clients. When evaluating processes, policies, and procedures through the lens of rich energy, you can recreate and reorganize new structures that support the company reality you want to create.

I have found that at tech companies, because the nature of their work is about innovation, there is a standard of high energy neutral as the baseline energy state. Companies such as Zappos and Facebook spend a good percentage of their time in energy rich and high energy neutral because the leaders have a worldcentric philosophy and have set up policies and processes to support an energy-rich work environment for employees as well as having an energy-rich customer-centric approach. For example one of the energy-rich structures that make Zappos what it is today is that they were at the forefront of free-shipping philosophy. When Zappos first introduced that concept to the market, there was huge concern that they would lose money. In fact Zappos created a new standard for the online industry overall that was followed by Amazon and other online retailers. This is what rich energy does; it adds energy to the entire system and, in this case, the focus was on adding value to the customer!

Last, after building awareness and reorganizing structures, you would begin to build performance evaluation systems, coaching systems, and collaboration systems based on levels of energy.

For individuals, there are opportunities to build further awareness about the energy states and the impact on personal performance. With the increased awareness, the focus would be on spending the majority of time thinking and behaving on the level of energy rich and high energy neutral. A CEO or a senior leader would want to strive to be energy-rich about 90 percent of the time to expand the field of energy for self and for the company. Minimally, the goal would be to increase the percentage of time spent in energy rich and high energy neutral each day, each week, each month, until the majority of your thinking, behaving, and the structures you create comes from an energy-rich perspective.

Actions to take to be in a consistent energy-rich state:

- Choose to elevate your thinking by focusing on what *can* be done, on positive and creative solutions .
- When you experience a setback or challenge, become aware of the fear, acknowledge the fear, and accept the

current reality; then choose a new compelling future bigger and better than what has been interrupted.

- See disruptions as necessary aspects of the cycle of life/work and learn to think energy-rich thoughts when you have a disruption, such as, "What opportunities does this disruption bring?" and "What can we create that is more sustainable and better?"
- Ask energy-rich questions such as, "What is the learning in this disruption?" and "What systems or structures can we change to create more growth and benefit for all?"
- Catch yourself when you are engaging in the blame game and shift immediately to taking personal responsibility and engaging others in brainstorming solutions.
- Engage in energy-rich activities that you know consistently *add* to your energy, such as exercise (for me its group classes as I enjoy being with people), meditation, yoga, being out in nature, listening to uplifting music, talking with someone who inspires you, watching inspiring videos. Make your own list and engage in those activities daily and weekly.

Think about those times when you achieved so much in so little time. Its not because you had become a master of time; it is because you had harnessed the power of being energy-rich.

There are many tools for transformation; the AQAL model and the energy states are just two of the potential transformational tools available. I believe that the future of work requires tools that are about focusing on worldcentric solutions and focusing on the amazing and untapped power of energy.

9

The Art of Adapting to Multiple Personalities, Different Generations, and Cultures

We seldom realize, for example, that our most private thoughts and emotions are not actually our own. For we think in terms of languages and images which we did not invent, but which were given to us by our society.

—Alan W. Watts

THE SINGLE MOST IMPORTANT FACTOR WHEN LEADING CHANGE

Throughout this book I have shared multiple perspectives on how you can be a transformer and how you personally can adapt to change. The single most important factor that I have found in my years of working with organizations and leaders is the ability to be an "uber adaptor." What is required, in addition to building your self-awareness and your personal change strategies, is that you must master the ability to connect with and relate to and influence others at the highest level possible. How do you do that?

You have to understand the many dimensions that make up an individual's approach to life and work. I mentioned earlier in the book that the future leader will have a prevalent attitude of being a humble leader and it is only in being consistently open to learning that one can be truly humble. A leader who, when leading change, has the combination of being humble by being a constant learner while also having the confidence of experience and skill, has the combination that is powerfully influential on others. People trust you when you are a lifelong student while also being a master teacher. Recently I had the pleasure of speaking to Mark Benson of E3 Wealth, and you will recall that earlier in the book I interviewed his colleague John. Mark is the leader who inspired John to be a "servant leader," and when I interviewed Mark he validated the success that comes from that approach.

The interview below shows the transformational mindset that Mark has had and continues to rely on to not only grow his own success (egocentric) but also grow the success of his entire team (ethnocentric) and further the desire to completely transform the financial services industry (worldcentric).

Interview of Mark Benson Ameritime

Cheryl: Your company is an industry leader because of your approach to add value for clients. From your perspective, what is different about your approach?

Mark: I have personally sat in on thousands of meetings with clients, and I discovered that financial professionals could do so much more to help people than how we were and how we are.

Cheryl: How do you specifically do more?

Mark: We provide a completely different approach and models to bring superior value to our clients. We focus on better education; we do a thinking exercise by having the client *think* differently about money. There needs to be better team work among financial professionals and they need to *stop* seeing their role as giving opinions and advice but, rather, wait until there is a fuller understanding of what the clients are *really* saying. We decided to turn the current financial-professional-approach model on its head. We want to be the leaders of change not just for our clients *but for the entire system/industry.*

Cheryl: So wanting to change the system for the industry is a world-centric approach and definitely creates more energy in the entire system. What are some ways you are changing the industry?

Mark: We have seen a huge lack in the industry of financial professionals being focused on *adding value* to clients. We have come at it backward and flipped the model on its head. The entire industry has been built on creating fear in the minds of clients. The fear of never having enough money creates a fear of managing wealth overall. We have redefined wealth as having freedom rather than accumulating wealth because of fear.

Cheryl: Can you give more examples of your change approach?

Mark: For example the financial industry norm teaches people to do a budget, which is an approach that focuses on what we can't have, which is a fear and scarcity approach. Instead, we do a thinking exercise to stop teaching and get people to think—a cash-flow-awareness thinking exercise versus a budget. The old model teaches people to accumulate, which is a never-ending and nonsatisfying approach. When will enough money ever be enough? That mind-set creates unhappy people! By focusing on cash-flow awareness and their quality of life,

(Continued)

we free up energy and excitement for what our clients' money *can do for them, not* how much they have in their bank balance, which is not psychologically satisfying. This is why we know many wealthy people who have spent a lifetime focused on accumulating and meanwhile they have lousy family relationships or they are miserable but they have all kinds of money. We want people to have fuller and richer lives that money helps them to *create*. Therefore, we are flipping the model that has been used in our industry. A not so secret of a secret that the public knows is that financial professionals are taught to teach people how to accumulate, which is tied to the financial planners' compensation. Customers no longer trust the professionals because their advice is tied to their compensation. By becoming partners and allies with our clients we have set it up that *they* set the fees based on what they determine are the ways in which we can best serve them. This is a transformative approach to the industry overall.

Cheryl: What you are saying is really ringing true with me as my corporate background is in finance and what you say about compensation tied to financial-company goals rather than the client was my experience when I was a financial professional. Would you say that this will be a difficult change for financial professionals to make?

Mark: Yes, and the market is already proving to financial professionals that clients are no longer willing to follow advice. They are far more informed and are looking for partners, not advisors. Clients who accumulate want to keep growing. We focus on not *just* accumulation; we focus even more on utilization, which is a complete change. I have a quick story about a client/friend who we gifted with tickets to a softball game and the client was so touched to have an amazing father/son day. The sad part of that story is that they have the money to have season tickets and their money thinking is that they have to keep accumulating and cannot *use* their money. That is just plain sad!

Cheryl: How else are you being transformers in the industry?

Mark: We are focusing on generational thinking involving three generations in the financial discussions process. This is unprecedented, as previous generations such as the Traditionalists have had a closed approach to their money. Our approach since we focus on utilization is to bring all family members to the table and talk about LIFE. We get them all talking about how to create abundance for the entire lineage through the utilization of money. We sit with multiple generations of our clients and bring in their attorneys and other professionals and we communicate openly about all things to do with money and quality of life and building wealth that is long-term and will thrive for generations to come.

Cheryl: That seems so obvious and yet as you say it's the fear of loss that prevents the open approach. What is one way the generations approach has worked well for you and your clients?

Mark: We have found that open communication among generations is so crucial to success. There is a book called *Rags to Rags* that goes into depth about how generations of wealth are typically lost after the third generation. Our approach is to extend the wealth in a family long-term by having a generations approach to money management.

(Continued)

We talk about where your money is going to go and what you can be doing now. One approach that works really well with our family clients is the concept of family bank and loaning money to family members at benefit to the family and at much lower rates than credit cards or loans.

Cheryl: Whether you know it or not, you have a world-centric approach to your business in that you have a huge vision to transform the industry overall; what are your ideas to do that?

Mark: We feel the need to help all financial professionals and an ideal model for us is to do an educational event for financial professionals—expanding on what financial professionals do. We want to help financial professionals create more value for clientele by adhering to our model that is proven to help grow a financial advisor practice.

We consider our approach the ideal model for our industry—and we have not found it yet elsewhere so we created it—and it is to bring an integrated network of financial professionals to specific markets to using a teamwork approach. The industry is so individualistic and we focus on bringing people together. Based on our success we want to create an integrated resource network to the entire industry.

We are starting this by offering events to financial professionals who we see as *co-opetition*—not competitors—to begin seeding these new approaches to the industry. Coopetition is future-focused on building success for all. Our approach and models have already increased financial planners' businesses by 30 percent in 19 months. In addition to educating our clients, we see an opportunity to educate the industry overall. This will transform business for the entire profession and increase value for clients overall.

Cheryl: Let's talk about you as a leader for a bit. Have you always been a leader that focuses on transformation?

Mark: That's a tough one in that I don't really know how to answer that. I came up with the strategy triangle using unique ability teamwork in the late 1980s and early 1990s when I was a high-school football coach. Didn't know anything about anything other than being a coach (I really wanted to be a coach). We won two state championships, worked hard, and had a lot of enthusiasm. I was pretty young to be coaching early on—first leadership role was 24 years old as head football coach, at age 27 coach of the year in Missouri. Winning really is a team effort, and then, at age 28, I was head football coach for another high school. Being a coach was phenomenal exposure to leadership. Then, when I was 33 years old, I got into financial services business, and my background as a math teacher and coach was perfect for the financial-services industry. Soon I was making more money in financial services than I was in my teaching/coaching career, and I shifted careers. My strengths finder (First Find Your Strengths Personality Indicator) indicated that I had innate leadership skills and good leadership skills as well as that I am competitive in things that I am good at. I would say that is accurate.

John Moriarity founder of E3 Wealth (a mentee of mine) and I have a similar focus and are a great team, and we have had lots of failures and lots of things that didn't work. We have spent lots of money on how not to do it and we are now in a position to further

(Continued)

transform the business. The key skills that help us to harness transformation are client-focused innovations in investment, creative approaches to money management, and cash-flow-thinking exercises.

Cheryl: You seem to have mastered the one thing that I say all leaders of change need to do and that is valuing and adapting to people. How do you do that?

Mark: Well I think I have been more focused on benefiting other people and overhauling the system, rather than focusing on myself. I often say that the leadership required to lead for these new times is leadership that consists of humility and confidence. I notice leaders and put them in the category of the can-do's and those that have the combination of being both humble and confident—people are not going to last without that. I have learned to share the knowledge and share what I know. Our company does not treat employees as employees but as partners. In fact, we have asked our people to make a list of the stuff they don't love to do and we have committed to provide them with support by having people do the stuff that they love. My philosophy is that if we get rid of the stuff you don't like to do, you will never want to retire! Our core group of about a dozen of us are superstars, and then 25 good people. These people are good people. I value people and I value the diversity that each person brings to the table.

It is clear from the interview with Mark that he is an uber adaptor, and he has attracted and retained a team of people who are also uber adaptors. What I enjoyed the most about interviewing Mark was the congruency of his approach, how he himself models and epitomizes the very approach that he inspires others to adopt.

At the end of the interview, Mark says that he values people, and when the focus is on appreciating and valuing people, there will always be an approach of adding value to others.

BE AN UBER ADAPTOR TO OTHER PEOPLE'S PERSONALITIES

Mark also mentioned using personality tools such as Strengths Finder (www.strengthsfinder.com/home.aspx), which I have used and I have facilitated for clients. It is one of many resources for better understanding your own strengths and personality strengths. Other models that I have used are the DISC system (www.thediscpersonalitytest.com/?view=Assessments_disc& gclid=CMqDz4fi-8QCFYZffgod_TEAEA) and there are others available. The ability to leverage what you know about your own style is valuable and the real and marked value is being able to increase your ability to adapt to others quickly, effectively, and with the focus to being able to collaborate and innovate. I have been working with personality profiles for over 20 years, and in my very first book, *Say What You Mean—Mean What You Say* (Trafford 2001) I presented my version of the personalities that I had called the four Ds.

The four Ds stand for:

Driver
Dancer
Detailer
Deflector

My version is not a comprehensive approach; rather, it's an at-a-glance tool that allows you to quickly identify others' personality styles and then choose a quick customized approach when speaking with others, in your writing to others, or engaging within a team.

The at-a-glance identifiers of the four Ds are shown in Table 9.1.

For a complimentary copy of the personalities chart go to www.cherylcran.com/personalitieschart.

The importance of being able to quickly adapt to different personalities cannot be overstated. When I mentioned earlier that change leaders need to be lifelong learners, this applies to those times when we have an attitude of "been there done that." I have been teaching personality styles for two decades and I am *still* learning more and more about how to *apply* what I have learned rather than just believe I know it all already, theoretically. So you may already know your own personality type because you have done other types of personality testing, and I ask you to review and then *do* the actions at the end of this section to elevate the application of what you know. Let's first confirm what you know about yourself. You will be the two styles that are opposite to the ones that least describe you. Keeping in mind that even as you develop your personality and you become more and more integrated with all four styles (which is the ultimate goal) you will still lead your life from two primary styles.

In my case, no matter what personality profile I do, I always come out as a Socializer (Dancer) and a Driver, and I have been working with these concepts to further develop and integrate my Detailer (Analytical) and my Deflector (Amiable). The more that you can develop your areas that are not your primary styles, the more ease you will have when interacting with others. Again, using myself as an example, when I first learned about my styles in my early 20s, I was clearly an underdeveloped version of Dancer/Driver in that I had to focus on the areas of improvement in order to develop my strengths. Now, at the stage I am in life (age) and time of application of the concepts (experience), I have developed the strengths of all four

Table 9.1   Four Ds identifiers

Driver Strengths	Dancer Strengths
Fast talking/fast-paced	Social and friendly
Direct and to the point	Big picture focus
Visionary and fast acting	Inspiring and engaging
Bold and willing to risk	Visionary and creative
Focused and results oriented	Influential and loves change
Areas to Improve	**Areas to Improve**
Impatient	Great starter/needs to finish
Blunt	Can be "Pie in the Sky"
Too results focused	Change for change's sake
Can be insensitive	Can overpromise
Language to use with a Driver	**Language to use with a Dancer**
I will get right on that.	Let's make it fun.
Consider it done.	What do you see for the future?
How soon would you like this?	Let's brainstorm.
What's the overall outcome you want?	How can we change this for a great outcome?
Detailer Strengths	Deflector Strengths
Analytical	Cares for people
Critical thinker	A great listener
Attention to detail	Intuitive
Plans and structures	Collaborator
Project management	Team player
Areas to Improve	**Areas to Improve**
Can make slower decisions	Can be overly sensitive
Can belabor the facts	Afraid to make decisions
Risk averse	Risk averse
Can be overly critical	Can be too nice
Language to use with a Detailer	**Language to use with a Deflector**
I gave this a lot of thought.	Let's make sure this helps people.
I researched this.	This will be appreciated by the people you work with.
I gathered data.	You are a great help.
Here is a report, spreadsheet, overview in writing.	How can we ensure that the team is on board with this?

quadrants to a pretty high degree. AND I am still learning every time I interact with anyone!

The key to leveraging personality styles to lead change and drive transformation is that it is a quick way to upgrade your operating system and to bring people along with you rapidly.

Recently I had a conversation with a potential client about working together. This client was clearly a Driver/Detailer and I instantly noted mentally that I would need to give this person both a direct response and a detailed response. I spoke in short and to the point sentences, I pointed out the results he would achieve and the company would achieve, and I promised to follow up with a detailed e-mail and proposal to support our discussion. As a result, the client agreed to bring me in to consult on a major project. In the past, I would have easily been able to speak to his Driver personality as it is one of my top two styles, but I would have completely avoided his need for detail because I would have perceived it as too much work! Clearly that approach has cost me business in the past. I have forced myself to learn how to be more analytical, to follow up in writing and to *honor* the needs of an analytical person. The result of investing my time and energy into developing this side of my personality is that I now have much better relationships with Detailers because I have learned to respect and value his or her strengths. Also, by better understanding the Detailers, I have learned to speed up decisions and relate and connect very quickly. Another example is a consulting client I have. She is a CEO of a major bio-tech firm and she is a Deflector/Detailer. When I first met Sheila, it was at a leadership event, and I instantly could see her discomfort at being in a big gathering and knew her primary style was a Deflector. I approached her with a friendly smile and a handshake and casually made a joke about "these types of gatherings." She visibly relaxed, and when

I told her what I did as a consultant, she immediately decided to hire me. In my early career, I had nothing but impatience for Deflectors, I found them too nice and unable to make decisions quickly. This, of course, did not work in my favor as I alienated the Deflectors around me with my gruff style at the time. With dedicated focus and a real desire to better connect with Deflectors I have come to truly appreciate their ability to connect with people, to care about people, and to "get more bees with honey." The result is that I can now bring on Deflectors within the companies I work as allies to support change initiatives and to leverage their abilities as influencers and sounding boards for the people on their teams. Sheila, my CEO Deflector client, values my natural Driver skills as she is further developing those skills in herself, and I enjoy supporting her and the processing that Sheila as a Deflector needs. This brief and Coles-notes version of personalities is to remind you that it is a very valuable tool as a driver of transformation: a tool that you are either using already or that you need to use and to master in order to being a master change leader. Here are eight questions to consider when leading change and getting people on board by adapting to their personalities:

1. Do you have a deep understanding of your own personality style?
2. Do you focus on the strengths of your personality and, as an ongoing humble student, are you learning how to better your areas for improvement?
3. Do you value the styles that are unlike your own?
4. Do you use the language of each of the styles to adapt to others more quickly?
5. Do you focus on identifying someone's personality style when you connect?

6. When you get frustrated or irritated by someone, do you stop to consider his or her personality style and how you have to adapt to them?
7. What can you do to become even more effective with dealing with diverse personalities?
8. Focus on practicing for the next few weeks on quickly identifying personality styles and then adapting to people using what you know. Monitor the results.

BE A MULTIGENERATIONAL MORPHER

In addition to further developing the personality adapting skills that are necessary to be an art-of-change leader you are likely also aware of or dealing with the multigenerational reality in the workplace.

A multigenerational morpher is someone who has developed the ability to recognize the diverse generational attitudes and someone who values differences and can adapt his or her approach based on this ability. I mentioned my book *101 Ways to Make Generations X, Y, and Zoomers Happy at Work* and it is a great resource on better understanding the different attitudes as it relates to time, seniority, work/life integration, and more. With the influence of technology and changing generational attitudes in the fast-paced workplace, reality, life, and work is never going to be the same. Having the skill to be able to identify generational approaches and then adapt your communication, leadership, and systems to this reality is part of the success factor for driving transformation.

My method of identifying the generations is to use age groups versus the years that the people were born. There are varying approaches to the generational research; demographers will focus very specifically on the years that each generation was born and there is even discrepancy between demographers on what constitutes each of the generational segments. I prefer a simple and easy-to-understand method that helps you to quickly identify a person's generation and then be able to factor in the generational attitude and values when interacting.

See Table 9.2 for easy identification.

As you can see from Table 9.2, there are wide ranges of influence within each demographics' upbringing and environments that helped to shape their attitudes and values. With the technological impact and the speed with which things are changing, a lot of the values are shifting for *all* the generations. Let's be clear that my approach is not to put people into boxes or to come at generations from an ageist perspective. You can be a Zoomer (a baby boomer who refuses to age—see www.zoomermag.com) who is more like a Gen Y, and you could be a Gen X or Y who is more like a Traditionalist or a Zoomer. The key use of the generations' information is to build awareness and adaptability skills to better relate to the diverse generations in the workplace.

In order to be a multigenerational morpher, you *must* learn to appreciate what has shaped the attitudes of each generation and, even more important, to approach each generation with that awareness. There is a new language that is emerging as a result of the major influence that Gen Y is having on the workplace.

I wrote a blog post about how to get best results when communicating with Gen Y. Here's an excerpt: "Research has shown that Gen Ys (those in their 20s to early 30s) do not respond to the criticism that many Traditionalists and Zoomers have had to endure. However Gen Ys do respond to coaching, feedback, and skill development aka 'honey'."

Table 9.2   Values of the Generations

Values of a Traditionalist (Late 60s and older)	Values of a Zoomer (early 50s to late 60s)
Traditional	Rebellious
Respect elders	Thought they would work until retirement
Loyalty to employer	Therapy and getting in touch with feelings
Seniority and line of command	Work hard and then you die
Task oriented	Both parents work to give to our children
Don't question authority	Loyal to employer to a degree
Don't spend more than you make	Indulged their children
Don't show emotions	Don't want to wait for nice things
Hard work	Take more risks
Law and order	Learned on the job
(Events included World War II and the Great Depression)	(Events included TV, Civil Rights Movement, prosperity, they value health and wellness, personal growth, and involvement)

Values of a Gen Y (20s to early 30s)	Values of a Gen X (mid 30s to early 50s)
The indulged generation	Fighting to be heard as they are squeezed between boomers and Gen Y
Highly creative	Creative and risk takers
Have never known life without technology	Family—take time for family
Do not want to leave home (they love their parents)	Work hard and then reality of family kicks in
Searching for the job they love	Waiting for the boomers to retire or promote them
Want to get the most out of each employer	Changed jobs at least 3–5 times in their working life
Change jobs at least a dozen times in their lifetime	Have been downsized and rightsized
Life first, work second	Want adventure and less structure
Do not give respect unless it is earned in their eyes	Want the perks
Want to have fun at work	Do not necessarily follow hierarchy
Loyal to people not employer	(Events included MTV, Watergate, and the Fall of the Berlin wall as well as the crisis in the early 1980s of high interest rates. They value diversity and global thinking)
(Events included school violence, terrorism, TV talk shows, You Tube, iTunes, and Guitar Hero)	

TALKING TO A GEN Y

In previous chapters I have mentioned the language to use with Gen Y and that the approach needs to be inspiring. The key item to remember when communicating/talking with a Gen Y is that they were raised by being praised. Most parents of Gen Y raised them with language such as, "you are special" or "you can do anything" or "don't be afraid to ask for what you want." With these messages Gen Y shows up in the workplace and expects to be "seen for his or her value" and to be spoken to in a way that is uplifting. Gen Y also do not respond well to direct criticism rather they respond to praise and feedback that will help them get to where they want to go quickly.

I have presented research on the generations for the past five years and, often, when I present the information on the attitudes and values of Gen Y, I will get questions from the audience such as, "Aren't the Gen Ys going to end up just like the Zoomers?"

My answer: No. The Gen Ys don't want to be anything like their parents and, because of technology, they don't have to be. Zoomers lived and worked in a time when in their young days they had to get a job to pay the bills and they did anything they were told in order to keep their jobs. Contrast that to the Gen Ys who were raised by the Zoomers and Gen X who, instead, are living at home longer, can start a business using their laptops or iPads, and who find more value in enjoying what they do rather than being obligated to do anything.

Which always leads to another question, which is, "Won't Gen Ys have to buckle down and get a real job once they start having families?"

My answer: No. Again, Gen Ys are the largest demographic that is entrepreneurial. A recent Fast Company survey showed that over 70 percent of Gen Ys would start their own business rather than work in a job or company that he or she didn't enjoy.

Typically, at that point someone sarcastically points out that they are using their parent's money to start a business and, although that may be true for some, many Gen Ys have creatively turned to sites like kickstarter.com and other funding sites to get their business ideas off the ground.

Right now, if you are reading this and you feel frustrated by the Gen Y attitudes, is it because it seems that things are easier for them? This comes back to what we have covered in previous chapters about creating organizations that continue to reorganize at higher and higher levels and that are focused on being energy rich. The Gen Y attitude goes with this approach: generally Gen Ys don't feel you have to work hard the way their parents did, and they believe you can leverage technology to work smarter not harder and have a life too. Frankly, I love Gen Ys in that I believe that their prevalent attitudes are going to change the future workplace. As more and more Gen Ys come into the workplace, their influence is going to continue to shape how technology is leveraged, how to add value to customers, how to create a workplace that values work/life integration, and this, in my opinion, is all for the good.

The Gen Xs in the workplace right now are in a unique position to be drivers of transformation in that they comprise the generation between the Zoomers and the Gen Ys. If you are a Gen X reading this, you likely have already figured out that, in order to move the pace of change forward, you need to bridge the strengths of both the Zoomers and the Gen Ys. Gen Xs have the benefit of gaining experience through working with and under the systems created by the Zoomers as well as being on the leading edge of technological innovation. Where a Gen X could focus his or her energy in mastering the art of change leadership is to look at ways to creatively engage the abilities of each of the generations in the workplace.

A creative Gen X senior leader that I have as a client has come up with ideas such as using Yammer in the workplace as an internal social-media portal, using Work.com as a real-time performance-evaluation system that appeals to Gen Y (and appeals with use to the Zoomers), using gamification such as Axonify.com to create gaming for repetitive training modules such as learning safety protocols, and more. This Gen X leader is very talented at bringing the proven experience of the Zoomers and the knowledge to the Gen Ys who then are able to leverage technology to increase and improve on current successes. He also created Gen Y council groups that are focused on providing key insights on customer service improvement using technology, and they also provide learning pods for helping Zoomers/Gen X learn how to leverage the use of existing technologies.

Many Zoomers I work with are extremely technologically advanced and have become far more like Gen Ys when it comes to technological knowledge and application. In many companies, I still see a generational gap in that there are some Zoomer mindsets that are fixed on their own viewpoints and are having a challenging time adapting to the attitudes and values of Gen Ys. A lot of biases such as Gen Ys are lazy or do not know how to communicate face-to-face still exist. I conducted a Gen Y survey a few years back and asked them if they thought they were lazy or entitled and, unequivocally, the responses back from Gen Y were that they were not lazy rather they were looking at efficient ways to get things done and they worked when they enjoyed what they were doing. With regard to the entitlement bias, Gen Ys feel that many Zoomers and Traditionalists act entitled because of the time they have had on their jobs when, in fact, Gen Ys may not have time on the job but can do a job faster and more effectively, that is, in less time. In relation to the face-to-face item, Gen Ys consider Facetime and Skype as viable face-to-face communication. There is tremendous opportunity for change leaders to further enhance generational communication awareness because this is and will continue to be a key success strategy in transforming through change.

The other greatest impact on the ability to lead change and transform business is recognizing the impact that diverse cultures have on the future of business.

EMBRACE DIVERSE CULTURAL VALUES

At this stage, you have become even more aware of the importance of adapting to personalities and generations as you look to the future. Another crucial factor is adapting to the diverse cultures that make up the business. With the race for talent and the continuing worker-shortage challenge one of the major solutions has been to engage diverse cultures. A construction client I worked with in Ontario took advantage of a government program that allowed him to hire temporary workers from Europe. The company was investing in apprentice programs and had partnered with local colleges and universities to bring in new talent, and the skills gap became an overwhelming challenge. The only way my client could solve this dilemma was to hire skilled workers from another country.

At first, it was a big challenge because the workers spoke very little English and, although they had construction skills, the language gap was a problem. The leadership came up with a change leader solution. They set up their own internal English classes specifically focused on the language needed in construction! They also used translation apps on the smartphones to improve translation between workers on the job site.

Research points to more and more cultures being hired to make up for the worker shortage and, therefore, everyone must increase his or her cultural awareness and adapt accordingly.

I recently worked with a major airline group that had something like 30 different cultures within the company. They hired me to provide a training program on leadership and change, and it became quickly evident that there was a cultural intolerance that had been created. There were challenges in understanding each of the cultural approaches and it was causing communication breakdown.

We spent time on identifying the attitudes and values of diverse cultures and how to communicate and lead in a way that respected and honored diverse cultural approaches.

The future workplace is going to be a place of fast-paced dynamic change with multiple cultures, continuing generational values gaps, and varying personalities and approaches. The ability to develop your skills to become agile and adept at dealing with these factors is going to be the key differentiator for your success as a transformational driver of change.

10

The Three-Step Change Process Model to Leading Personal and Organizational Change

Netflix is now bigger than CBS #disruption

—Tweeted by @joannmoretti April 2015

EMBRACE THE DISRUPTION

Disruption is a big word being bandied about by technology firms and innovative company leaders. There is now a growing and global understanding that innovation cannot happen without disruption. Something needs to be disturbed and disrupted before it can transform to the next level. It also is a word that is now being rejected by tech firms as being on overused term.

The other evening my husband Reg and I were watching *Shark Tank* (I love that show because of the entrepreneur/ innovation mix) and there was a mother and son on the show proposing a product ... wait for it ... Squatty Potty. I hesitated in sharing this story in this book *but* it's a great example of disruption of a product and an industry. The mother on the team had discovered that as she was aging she needed a better solution for "doing her business" and invented the Squatty Potty. Turns out that about two-thirds of the world "goes" this way and it's healthier and better for you. The concept, of course, was titillating for media and embarrassing enough to get the attention of Dr. Oz where they promoted the product before appearing on *Shark Tank*. The Sharks all giggled nervously at the concept and it was Lori Greiner as the Shark that invested in the company. A few weeks later I am casually watching Dr. Oz one evening and there on the show was Lori and the mother/son duo talking to Dr. Oz about Squatty Potty and they were sharing how the sales have soared sky high. They had disrupted the plumbing industry! Disruption can come in many forms; it can be a disruptive product or service that is a game changer—think iPhone, Netflix, Uber—to an entire industry. Disruptions can also show up as in changing client habits, different wants and needs. An example, once again, is Kodak—the market and clients were going digital while Kodak was trying to hang on to the previous client behaviors of sticking with film.

Uber is a great example of disruption of an entire industry; wherever I travel throughout North America I have used Uber and I love the service. Of course, taxi and limo owners do not like the disruption that Uber has caused. Any time there is a structure that protects a system, you can bet that there will be resistance when something threatens that system. However, disruptions that are driven by consumer demands are hard to prevent or resist. In Vancouver, Canada, the taxi owners are adamantly against allowing Uber in the city. The irony is that there are not enough taxis to serve clients well and yet the taxi companies want to minimize consumer access to expanding driver services. Disruption doesn't stop when it is resisted; it happens based on the value it adds to consumers, and when people and companies do not embrace disruption or they resist, they try to thwart and they keep the system small rather than expanding. My sense is that Uber will eventually be in almost every city. Why? Because the consumer demands the service!

A similar disruptive model in an industry is Air BNB, the online short-term-stay service. Recently I was a keynote speaker for a hotel industry event in New York City. Another hotel industry speaker spoke on industry trends and showed that Air BNB is edging into hotel occupancy rates by over 30 percent. The hotel industry is looking at this disruption as an opportunity to compete with home-away-from-home features in their hotels, building more all-suite hotels and more.

Technology is disrupting every single industry out there; in manufacturing, robotics is quickly becoming a reality and is disrupting the model of how things are produced. The music industry has been disrupted with companies like Spotify and other streaming services. The publishing industry is being disrupted by online access to content, ebooks for ereaders, and consumers wanting merged content delivered in video, written format, and audio. The financial industry is being disrupted by online financial planning and financial management tools, which has caused financial planners/brokers to re-look at how they add value beyond being a provider of information. The insurance industry is being disrupted with services like Esurance and other online quoting solutions where the consumer controls their services. Even the entertainment industry is being disrupted with people choosing the media that interests them rather than turning on a TV with preset programming.

EMBRACING DISRUPTION IS A TOOL FOR TRANSFORMATION AND IS PART OF THE THREE-PART MODEL TO LEADING PERSONAL AND ORGANIZATIONAL CHANGE

Before we go into the model and the solutions or discuss how to use the model to navigate change, let's talk a bit about personal disruption. It is relevant to apply disruption to your personal reality because that is really at the crux of being an uber adaptor to change. The ability to *embrace* disruption and quickly respond and take proactive action when disruptions occur is a key skill for driving transformation as an individual. Think of your own life and work—think of a disruption that occurred. What did it mean to you? How did you react? What did you learn? What did it cause you to do differently? What were the gifts?

Your success is based on the level that you have developed disruption tolerance, the ability to be flexible and agile with disruption. You must build your agility muscles around disruption and you can then become a master transformer who can adapt much faster and speedier than ever before. You may have always been someone who could handle many disruptions and turn them to your and others' advantage or you may be someone who has had a higher need for certainty or stability and you have had low disruption tolerance. Either way, as a muscle you can build the muscle and then be able to flex and use it at will. Early in my career I left banking and then went to insurance; from there I went on to head up a mortgage program for a large credit union; they had never had a mortgage-area manager before and my role was to grow the mortgage business to $10 million in one year. The area was at about $5 million at the time. My partner and I achieved $10 million in 10 months, and they came to us and told us that we had oversold the mortgage portfolio and we no longer had jobs. This was 10 months after the previous downsize of the mortgage insurance company! Clearly this disruption was giving me a message. The credit union offered me a role as a branch manager and I turned it down because I knew that I would stagnate in that role. I had already been an assistant branch manager when I was with the bank and so I chose to leave. I came home to my husband and told him I quit my job and I was going to be an entrepreneur. I had no idea what I was going to do but I knew that the disruptions had happened for a reason. My dad was an entrepreneur before he passed suddenly when I was 20, and I remember thinking then that life was too short, and that thinking is what helped me to choose to be an entrepreneur. I left the credit union with the vision of using the disruption to become my own boss.

At around that same time, I met a business coach named Michael, and I studied with him for over a year before interning with his consulting firm for a year. Once the year of interning was over, I decided I was going to go out on my own. That was 1994 and I have never looked back. I have very high disruption tolerance but not because I am unique; rather, it is because I have *learned* to listen and watch for the messages of a disruption and then take proactive action.

It is because of my high disruption tolerance that I have chosen a field in which I must be the one disrupting, by providing provocative thinking, ideas, and challenging the norms. This book is a disruption!

Now back to you. What's your story?

What are your personal disruptions?

How have you leveraged and learned from them?

What will you do now that you have read this book and have recognized the opportunity to have even higher tolerance for disruption, change, and innovation?

What are the disruptions your industry is facing right now?

How is your company leveraging disruption to transform how you do business?

What is the disruption tolerance of your employees?

As a leader of change, are you helping others to see the value of embracing disruption?

Here are some steps to help you and your company embrace disruption as part of the three-step change model:

1. Assess yourself about your level of disruption tolerance by asking the preceding questions.
2. Assess your team's level of disruption tolerance by facilitating a discussion based on the preceding questions.
3. Assess your company's level of disruption tolerance by having the entire senior leadership group analyze the industry disruptions and how your company can be drivers of transformation in the industry by modeling disruption tolerance.

Once you have assessed and you have a sense of where you and your company are with disruption tolerance, you may want to consider building your findings into your strategic plans. You may also want to bring in a consultant/facilitator to help the senior leadership team to go deep with disruption tolerance analysis and build plans and strategies that support the growth and transformation goals for the company.

The next step/phase of the three-part model for change is to prepare yourself and others for the hero's journey. Once you have embraced the disruption and you have analyzed what it will take to be leading and driving transformation for the people, the company, and the industry, you now have to rally yourself and the troops to truly engage with the vision and to individually commit to the heroes journey.

COMMIT TO THE HERO'S JOURNEY

A hero is someone who has given his or her life to something bigger than oneself.

—Joseph Campbell, *The Hero's Journey*

The hero's journey is very familiar to many leaders. For most leaders and specifically change leaders, choosing to take the hero's journey is to see leadership as a superhero approach. The reality that a single person can change and influence the world is a pretty powerful pull toward a goal and objective. When the opposite thinking occurs, when someone believes that he or she is only one person and does not have the power to change anything or influence anything, then there is apathy and zero energy. Either belief can be a dominant thought. Which do you choose? Honestly.

As a change leader and a driver of transformation, you are likely to spend the majority of your time believing that what you say and do does make an impact, otherwise you wouldn't be in your current role nor would you be reading a book about driving transformation. Every story about heroes depicts the hero having his or her doubts at some stage of the journey or a "dark night of the soul," and then he or she chooses to reclaim his or her inner hero and forges ahead to drive transformation. In the three-part change model you *must* unequivocally be committed to your own hero's journey *and* also help to guide others to his or her journey *and* create a compelling outcome that will lead the entire company to a celebration.

Your own hero's journey can be seen as your personal desire to live your life and your work as a superhero story. Deepak Chopra wrote about this in his book, *The 7 Spiritual Laws of Superheroes*. The whole concept of superheroes really appeals to Generation X and Y, as it has been in their generation that there has been a big explosion of superhero movies. Generation X and Y are also the gaming generations in which the video games they have been playing since childhood are all about saving the world and getting points for winning as a hero.

Zoomers can connect to the Superman and Wonder Woman era of superheroes, which had appeal, and the Gen X and Y are looking at teams of superheroes being in the mainstream movies with movies like the X-Men and Guardians of the Galaxy. The superhero movies have shifted from one lone hero to teams of heroes each bringing his or her gifts to solve the world's problems.

How can *you* commit to the hero's journey? First you must see yourself and your work as having deeper meaning than just a job or just little-old you. Next, you have to commit to a mind-set that focuses on being a part of something that is far greater and has more far-reaching implications than you may have ever thought before.

A great exercise is to create a hero's journey map. This is an exercise that I guide leaders through when I facilitate workshops on change leadership. With the hero's journey map, you create a visual tool that shows where you are now and where you want to be in a given time frame. You plot out your challenges and your goals as things you want to access when you face certain roadblocks and you visually provide resources and reminders of what you will do when faced with roadblocks to the goals identified in the map. Access your hero's journey map template for free here www.cherylcran.com/heroesjourneymap.

Leaders of change and drivers of transformation create positive stories and mythologies that they use as an inspiring guidance tool and to help them remind themselves of the journey and the ultimate goals. You already know what thoughts and actions keep you motivated and focused on the goals and having visual tools to remind yourself and to refer to can help you stay focused on the resources you can access when you get challenged or feel defeated.

GET OTHERS TO COMMIT
TO THE HERO'S JOURNEY

There is no other way to motivate others to claim their hero's journey than for you to model it. When you model the commitment to growth and learning and the bigger vision, it cannot help but inspire others to want to do the same. Recently I conducted a survey of 200 leaders in the United States and one of the multiple-choice questions was, "In your role as a change leader, what do you find are your biggest challenges as they relate to leading change?"

Potential answers:

A. Getting all team members to buy into the vision.
B. Getting all team members to work at top performance levels.
C. Getting all team members to leverage technology.
D. Getting all team members to be more entrepreneurial and innovative.

Of the four possible answers, which do you think had the highest response?

The answer is B, getting all team members to work at top performance levels. Over 43 percent of the respondents said that B was their biggest challenge. This is relevant because it relates to inspiring others to commit to their journeys. When team members are connected to the "why" what they do is important and "why" they need to do their job at high performance levels and "why" they need to commit to the hero's journey, then they will step up. The many consulting clients I have worked with have confirmed that the biggest challenge is inspiring and leading top performance.

A potent solution is to help teams individually connect to their hero's journey as well as commit to the overall team goals as a team of heroes. The concept of hero's journey is not a tool to just get people to work harder. That would backfire because your teams would see it as another smoke and mirrors attempt at getting more out of them. It is crucial that the hero's journey is a full all-in commitment that includes reward and recognition and celebration as progress is made. You can set up the hero's journey as a fun and yet powerful way to have individuals engage and for the entire team and company to create energy while building toward the goals set out by the entire group of stakeholders.

One of the key components of keeping people engaged in future opportunities and in leading change is celebration. In my experience I have found this is where many leaders fall off. A lot of focus is on setting the plans, the goals, the timelines, and on what leaders want. There is less energy given for helping engage all team members in the hero's journey and typically even less energy to celebrate the milestones. The celebration is key, otherwise the whole focus of striving for results creates a team of people who become jaded, burned out, and losing energy.

CELEBRATE THE SUCCESSES

The evolution of the workplace and the massive change that is facing organizations is causing the need to celebrate even the small wins. Many tech start-ups understand this philosophy and start the business with celebration in mind. Traditional organizations may have a more challenging time creating a culture of celebration; however, it can be done. In fact, one of the ways for more traditional organizations to effect positive change is to shift the culture into a start-up mentality.

A client I have been working with for the past year recently developed with my help a new division and product delivery for his company. The company has been around for over 30 years and has succeeded with its current services, and now the CEO wants to expand delivery into new markets and opportunities. When we strategized the best way for his company to do this, one of the key agreements we needed all stakeholders to agree on was that this new direction/division needed to be treated as a start-up. By focusing on the new division as a start-up, everyone had to think like an entrepreneur and allow for slower starts and for people to fail along the way. Also, by putting the new division in a start- up category, it could be used as a laboratory for innovation for the other more traditional part of the business as well.

Start-ups in the tech industry know that there will be stops and starts to success and that celebrating milestones that are not just focused on results keeps the teams engaged and motivated for the long term. Frank Gruber, the author of *Startup Mixology*, devotes an entire chapter to the power of celebration for start-up companies, and his ideas apply to all companies. When creating your models for change and using the first two parts of the model, which is to embrace disruption and commit to the hero's journey, the third part of celebrating the successes is the anchor. If a leader or a company focuses on creating results without celebrating the aspects of the journey, people will feel undervalued and low energy neutral apathy will be quick to set in. A current consulting client in the natural products industry is going through massive change. The CEO is experiencing major market influences on the main products and they are in a middle of a lawsuit. The employees have been dealing with the challenges of providing superior customer service while dealing with restrictions and roadblocks because of the lawsuit. In other words they are treading water right now and cannot make much forward progress until there is movement on the lawsuit. In a leadership-team meeting I facilitated, we talked about the importance of keeping the entire team engaged and celebrating during this extremely difficult and stressful time. The COO and the director of operations agreed and have been planning activities and celebrations for progress that may appear as baby steps; for example, just recently the team came up with creative solutions for product delivery and the whole company went go-kart racing at the end of a work day in the middle of the week. The CEO has also taken the entire company to a team-building activity of creating office art together. The focus on continued celebration is of high value when going through massive change, and it is something that needs to be built into the ongoing activities. The norm is for most leaders and companies to only celebrate major wins but there can be major gaps between those events; celebrating events that are milestones keeps the gas in the tank for everyone.

A colleague of mine, Scott Friedman, has an entire book on celebration, titled *Celebrate—Lessons Learned From the World's Most Admired Organizations* and I encourage you to check it out for ideas and stories about the power of celebrating as a continual transformation tool for your team and company.

Here are six reasons why celebration can enhance transformation in your workplace.

1. **Ongoing celebrations provide consistent positive focus and energy.**

    Focus on all areas of an employee's hard work and accomplishments.

    For example, your team may have not reached the full quarterly target, but they secured a major lead that could double results next quarter. That could be celebrated.

In addition when a team does not meet dollar targets, it's an opportunity to debrief the facts and do a reality check about the products/services and the sales process itself. You could celebrate what was learned and celebrate the plan to exceed targets next quarter. Celebrating when results have *not* been achieved is counter to how many organizations currently operate. By creating a work environment of ongoing celebration for relevant reasons you create a workplace where people feel valued as contributors. When the culture is set up to reward only results, there can be a sense of feeling defeated because the targets always get moved upward. Celebrating the journey builds greater trust and teamwork and builds energy to go for the results consistently.

2. **Celebrations are a chance to give everyone a break.**

    Research has confirmed that Generations X and Y value time off and specifically when that time off can be shared with his or her family. For example if your teams have been going nonstop on a project and they finally make headway, be it minor or major, a great way to celebrate is to give everyone time off by letting them have a full day off or letting them leave early on a Friday. A construction company I worked with a few years ago took this to the next level by buying family outings for their employees such as dinner and a movie or recreational activities. This went over in a big way with the teams because they felt valued not just for the work that they did but also for the added value the company gave to their families.

3. **Celebrations are part of keeping your top talent.**

    We have established that ongoing change is the new norm for most companies. Every worker I have interviewed over the past 20 years or so has confirmed that the pace of change today is like being in a constant marathon. Celebrating provides those "water breaks" for the marathon. If you have ever participated in a race such as a 10 mile or a half marathon or a full marathon you know that those water breaks are necessary. Athletes know that replenishing the system is crucial to having stamina to finish the race. Think of mini celebrations and ongoing celebrations as the key elements of reaching goals and targets and creating the changes needed for business success.

A lot of companies have a culture in which all employees just go at top speed and then they burn out, get sick or crash. Building celebrations into the mix lessens the likelihood of sick days and crashing. Companies that celebrate have less challenge with attendance and less chance of people leaving for competitors.

An interesting note on retention: Many employees are planning to leave their current employers even when they are happy where they work. This is part of the rapid change of demographics and global opportunity that has the Generation X and Y always looking for the next best option. In India, for example, a 2012 Mercer survey highlights that no fewer than 54 percent of Indian workers are seriously considering leaving their jobs, and that figure spikes to 66 percent in the 16–24-year age bracket. Other independent studies confirm the correlation between intention to leave and actual turnover. The really tricky part is that the people considering leaving are not even desperately unhappy. Seventy-six percent of Indians surveyed reported satisfaction with their jobs and 75 percent with their organizations

Think of ongoing celebrations as a part of your overall employee retention strategy in addition to being part of the ongoing change leadership focus of your company.

4. **Celebrations will elevate the fact that you are a fun place to work.**

Don't laugh—a fun company is a company that people want to work for. There are many "best companies to work for" who have built the fun factor into their operations in order to increase the ability to attract and retain employees. Companies like Google, Twitter, and Zappos have focused on fun cultures as part of their strategy. Generation Y specifically is attracted to leaders and companies that are relaxed, that have some fun aspect to the job, and that celebrate along the way.

Each year, the Great Place to Work Institute asks tens of thousands of employees to rate their experience of workplace factors, including, "This is a fun place to work." On Fortune's "100 Best Companies to Work For" list, produced by the Great Place to Work Institute, employees in companies that are denoted as "great" responded overwhelmingly—an average of 81 percent respond that they are working in a "fun" environment. That's a compelling statistic: Employees at the best companies are also having the best time. At the "good" companies—those that apply for inclusion but do not make the top 100, only 62 employees out of 100 say they are having fun.

5. **Celebrations create a story for your customers.**

"No one cares about your story more than you do," writes Gruber in *Startup Mixology*. Celebrating events such as company anniversaries can create a story about your brand to your customers.

Storytelling, as most brands use it, is often a one-way street, in which the brand tells the story to potential customers. Involving the entire company in brainstorming celebration ideas as well as creating opportunities for employees to share his or her story about working for your brand in a celebratory way can add value to your brand in a few ways. First, it shows outside potential employees that the company is fun and inclusive, and second, it provides a story to your market about how you engage at work to provide services and products to the consumer. People want to do business with companies that have stories and are having fun while they are working hard for the customer. A tech firm I recently consulted with had an anniversary celebration at which they had photo booths and video stations at the event and encouraged employees and clients to "share their story" about the company. The photos and videos were shared via the Intranet within the company and, with permission, some of the photos and videos were made viral on social media. The employees loved the fun nature of sharing and the customers got to experience the fun that the tech company has at work and participate with the brand in a new and different way.

6. **Mini celebrations create opportunities for spontaneous fun.**

Spontaneous celebrations can be incredibly motivating and create an energy-rich environment quickly. For example a manufacturing client of mine had her warehouse manager suggest in the middle of the day that he take the warehouse team outside for a 30-minute game of soccer in the back parking lot. At first she balked, and then the warehouse manager upped the ante by setting a production goal that, if achieved in an hour, *then* they would go out for a 30-minute game. My client agreed and the team exceeded the goal the warehouse manager set by 30 percent. Everyone was happily surprised *and* the warehouse manager continued to create spontaneous celebrations and activities at intervals such as every few weeks or a few weeks in a row.

Celebrations and having fun can be part of the culture, and when it is top of mind for everyone, it can contribute to getting more people to perform at higher levels. Having fun and celebrating are essential tools especially for companies working at fast paces and dealing with ongoing change.

To review the three-step change process model for personal and organizational change:

1. Embrace disruption.
2. Commit to the hero's journey.
3. Celebrate the successes.

These three aspects are a continual cycle similar to the change cycle—you will rotate through them. Just as you have celebrated a success, you will have to embrace the next disruption and then you will have to gather the strength and resources to recommit to the hero's journey and then you celebrate the successes and so on.

Every idea and story I have shared in this chapter applies to you on a personal level. Your ability to model and lead the three-step change process will be the biggest positive impact on those you lead and influence. I recently realized that I personally was doing a good job of embracing disruption and committing to the hero's journey but I was not being consistent with celebrating.

Like you and many others, I am so focused on getting things done and constantly striving to be agile and future-focused that I was not taking time for fun.

Once I recognized that this was missing I recommitted to adding some fun time into my workdays as well as spontaneously inviting my co-workers to a quick game, take in a spontaneous movie, or play with my dog, Bob, the Yorkie.

There will be areas of leading change that will be easier for you than other areas. As you build your awareness, you will become more vigilant about ensuring you are using the resources available to you including items such as this book to remind you.

11

Thrive While Driving Transformation That Changes the World

Today, companies have to radically revolutionize themselves every few years just to stay relevant. That's because technology and the Internet have transformed the business landscape forever. The fast-paced digital age has accelerated the need for companies to become agile.

—Nolan Bushnell

SURVEY SAYS...

The future is either something you anticipate with positive expectation or it is something you fear because of the uncertainty or the unknown.

As stated previously in this book, when you focus on consistent reorganization, you are eagerly awaiting the future, you prepare for it, and you have positive expectation that the future will be even better than the past and the present. However, if you focus on the past as *the* only place where you were happy and if you focus on the past as a source of pain, then you are operating in a restore approach. This entire book has been written to help you to reorganize at higher levels than before. The goal that I set out when I envisioned this book was to provide a transformational guidebook for leaders and teams to take a hold of individual ability to drive transformation. A company is an organism, and a fully functioning organism ensures that all of its parts are working together toward a common purpose. I prepared a survey for this book that was sent out to over 250 leaders in the United States, which asked them 10 questions that speak to the existing challenges that leaders face as they relate to leading change, and it also focuses on leaders' perspectives on the future workplace.

All of the questions were multiple choices, and I will share the results here along with my thoughts on the responses. The survey answers provide further confirmation of the research I have conducted and studied over the past two decades. See how you align with the survey responses, and then follow the suggestions and ideas I provide as well as any ideas you self-generate.

Survey April 2015 of 250 Leaders in U.S. Companies

Question 1: In your opinion, what is the main cause of the fast pace of change that companies are experiencing right now?

Multiple Choice Answers/Responses
a. Technological Innovation: 31.4 percent.
b. Younger demographics in the workplace: 5.31 percent.
c. Increasing global competition: 9.18 percent.
d. All of the above: 54.11 percent.

In a larger survey conducted by IBM in 2012, the majority of the respondents indicated technological innovation was the biggest cause for the speed of change. This survey confirms this with 31.4 percent stating that they believe it is technology forcing the change. Interestingly only 5.31 percent feel that it is the younger demographics and 9.18 percent feel it is global competition, whereas 54.11 percent of the respondents cited all three factors of technology, demographics, and global competition that are the reason for the fast pace of change. In your company what would you say is the cause, and think of specific examples?

Economist Insights report on the future business in 2020 states that few industries will remain untouched by technological innovation. Their survey indicates that six out of 10 business leaders fear that their business will not exist by the year 2020.

Andrew McAfee, a principal research scientist at the MIT Sloan School of Management (MIT, United States), believes that major technology advances are still coming. "The kinds of developments we're seeing now are no longer the stuff of science fiction," he says. "We have never before had computers that could reliably recognize speech as we're talking, process it, and give answers back to us in real time. We have never before seen a computer that could beat the all-time best human being in a TV quiz show. And we have certainly never seen cars that could drive themselves on roads in traffic."

It is important to note that, with technology as a major factor in the fast pace of change, although a revolutionary technology may emerge, it is more likely that disruption will be caused by a technology that is already in existence and that is applied in new ways, whether to radically improve business processes themselves or to develop more innovative means of interacting with customers. The changes coming will be more about business models, and how technology is being used to change an organization and its impact on customers, rather than some major technology change on its own. We will see more fusion of technologies with examples such as Facebook's purchase of WhatsApp and Instagram as well as Google's ongoing foray into futuristic technologies such as Google Goggles and the driverless car.

The demographics and global changes are impacts, as I have shared earlier. Generations Ys are the innate users of technology and are playing a major part in the use of technology to innovate business. Globalization is impacting all business as volumes of business shift from the West to the East, and the speed of this change will continue to increase as demand in developing countries stands to exceed volumes of Western countries.

With the survey response given earlier, we can conclude that the biggest impact on the fast speed of change is technological innovation.

The next question I had shared in Chapter 10, and I provide additional perspective here to include it in the overall survey.

Question 2: In your role as a leader, what do you find are your biggest challenges as it relates to leading change?

Multiple Choice Answers/Responses
   a. Getting all team members to buy into the vision: 29.95 percent.
   b. Getting all team members to work at top performance levels: 42.51 percent.
   c. Getting all team members to leverage technology: 9.66 percent.
   d. Getting all team members to be more entrepreneurial and innovative: 17.87 percent.

No surprise here, in my opinion, because leading change requires the focus and commitment to engage people in the process. The top response of 42.51 percent saying that getting all team members to work at top performance levels is their biggest challenge in leading change. The performance level of all team members is the single biggest factor as it relates to your company's ability to be speedy and agile with change.

These results confirm that the entire way that performance is measured and reviewed needs to be transformed. I believe that one of the reasons that getting people to perform is an ongoing challenge is because leaders need to further develop their skills at coaching/guiding and inspiring their people to top performance. In addition to improving leaders' abilities, there needs to be an overhaul to the structures that are used to evaluate performance and reward performance. I mentioned real-time performance feedback as one mechanism that can assist with this (such as www.work.com) as a way of shifting and changing employee performance away from old systems of an annual performance review toward modern technological solutions that provide real-time data and information to recognize and reward performance more readily.

Question 3: In your company would you say that the overall culture as it relates to leading and managing change is:

Multiple Choice Answers/ Responses
   a. Everyone is eager to move forward and create next level of success: 10.63 percent.
   b. Most of the employees are on board with a small percentage not on board: 27.05 percent.
   c. There is a push-pull happening where we make progress and then we have to get everybody back on board: 33.82 percent.
   d. We have a large group of people who do not see any benefit in changing at all (if it ain't broke, don't fix it): 28.5 percent.

The responses to this question were close with b: most employees are on board with a small percentage not on board, equating to about a quarter of the respondents, followed by d at a slightly higher percentage. We have a large group of people who do not see any benefit in changing at all. The respondents who answered d have a big challenge ahead as they likely responded to the biggest challenge as a leader is getting people to buy into the vision. If your company has a large group of people who don't want to change, there needs to be a big focus right now on creating a compelling future, gaining individual buy-in, and aligning performance with reward and recognition. A company that does not address the resistance or fear of change with their large group of people runs the risk of not being able to stay competitive in the long run. The very viability of the company is at risk, and this includes union shop, government, or private. There are so many options arising because of technological innovation that any company that does not have the people on board to move forward will be met with fierce competition and solutions as mentioned throughout this book. Quick reminder: taxi industry and Uber . . . .

The largest response to this question was answer c; there is a push-pull happening where we make progress and then we have to get everybody back on board, with 33.82 percent choosing this multiple choice answer. If this is your answer, too, then you are in better shape than those who answered with d. Having a push-pull is a completely natural part of the change and transformation cycle. However, there is an opportunity to maximize the flow of transformation by reassessing and monitoring people's level of engagement and buy-in on a daily basis. Often there is a complacency that sets in once changes have been accepted and teams are integrating the changes in their daily work. It's a bit of a restore mentality that sets in and an energy neutral resting place. This is where leaders of change and transformation need to up the ante and generate more energy richness so that there is a higher set point that results in less of the push-pull and more of a consistent flow of innovation and energy as you and your team innovate and create. You can assess the patterns within your teams of when apathy may begin to set in and increase the fun factor while engaging the team to innovate ways to stay energy-rich and excited about the goals and the focus for the future. Leaders can benefit from adding the recognized cycles of when team energy can become low and add this information to the timelines or project management plan and focus on spending more one on one time with all of the individuals on the team to ensure they have the resources they need, as well as provide inspiration and support.

Question 4: Does your company have a clear focus on driving transformation such as increasing client value and creating a workplace of choice?

Multiple Choice Answers/Responses
   a. Yes, we are innovators and we value and reward innovation: 16.43 percent.
   b. Yes, and we are striving to have more of our company teams on board with this focus: 38.16 percent.
   c. No, we are so busy dealing with the current business and projects that we are not as focused on the future as we should be: 31.88 percent.
   d. No, we are focused on protecting the business we do have and ensuring we can maintain our current level of customers: 13.53 percent.

The good news to the responses to this question is that there are more leaders who answered a, yes we are innovators and we value and reward innovation than those who answered d, no, we are focused on protecting the business we do have and ensuring we maintain our current levels of customers. For those leaders who answered d, the leadership focus needs to radically shift away from protecting the business and toward reorganizing the focus on adding increased value to customers and employees so that the result is increased business not maintaining. Maintaining is energy poor, as I shared in previous chapters, and it is a sure indicator that the overall business will be in risk for its future viability if you or your leadership team do not take swift and energy-rich action right away. It's good news that 38.16 percent are striving to have more on board with driving transformation, because this is the key to the business thriving and growing in the near and long term. For you, if would choose this answer as well, your energy needs to be focused on getting more people on board, engaging more time on repeating the vision and the rewards to all of the stakeholders. The answer c, no, we are so busy dealing with the current business and projects that we are not as focused as we should be, is also a red flag that indicates being "busy being busy" is detracting from a focus on setting up systems and structures to ensure that the focus is equally on future and driving transformation as it is on maintaining the business.

You may have heard of the Jim Collins book *Good to Great*. In it he provides evidence and rationale as to why "good is the enemy of great," because many will settle for good enough rather than focus on a consistent great. The purpose of this book is to provide ideas and inspiration to focus consistently on great and amazing and extraordinary.

Question 5: When it comes to the performance of your teams and how they lead change would you say:

Multiple Choice Answers/Responses
   a. We have amazing teams of people who are eager to create results, work well together, and support each other's success: 15.46 percent.

b. We have teams of people who say all the right things and really want to create results but there are personality clashes and power struggles slowing down progress: 39.61 percent.

c. We are working to provide resources and tools to our teams to better equip them to be more innovative and to be rewarded for leading change: 28.99 percent.

d. We have teams who are very reluctant to take positive action because our culture has not rewarded decision-making or innovation up until this point: 15.94 percent.

The responses to this question resulted in the top percentage of 39.61 percent to be for b, we have teams of people who say all the right things and really want to create results but there are personality clashes and power struggles slowing down progress. I think this answer confirms one of the top concerns of CEOs, which is the impact that conflict has on overall productivity and innovation. The leaders who chose this as their answer in this survey have a big opportunity to invest in training and coaching and facilitating communication improvement, conflict management skills, and personality style awareness. Think about the amount of time that is wasted when people are not able to work together effectively. Leaders that drive transformation need to provide the resources and skill building to help people develop his or her people skills, and this survey response validates the necessity of spending both time and money on this particular area. The good news is that answer a had 15.46 percent of the respondents that said that they have amazing teams of people who are eager to create results, work well together, and support each other's success. Fantastic! This means the leaders are leading change and driving transformation in those companies. I would venture a guess that those respondents are enjoying great business success with consistent energy and productivity among their teams.

The 28.99 percent that responded with answer c, we are working to provide resources and tools to our teams to better equip them to be more innovative and to be rewarded for leading change, are also in pretty good shape. The fact that they are focused on providing resources and tools demonstrates they are willing to invest the things needed in order to set up their people and teams for greater success. Finally the 15.94 percent who responded with d, we have teams who are very reluctant to take positive action because our culture has not rewarded decision-making or innovation up until this point, have a bigger project ahead of them. There is an entire culture transformation needed for those leaders and their companies who chose this response. I would hazard a guess that these companies are traditional and long-standing and have had an embedded cultural norm of tight control from the top down. There is a transformation of the culture needed to move away from control and command and toward all-employee-level decision-making and an entrepreneurial approach that is rewarded.

> **Question 6:** Technology as a major game changer is a differentiator between companies that are both productive and profitable. How would you say your teams are at staying abreast of technological innovation and leveraging technology to improve business?

Multiple Choice Answers/Responses

> a. Our teams are highly technologically savvy and are consistently on top of technological innovation and how to leverage technology to improve our business: 17.39 percent.

b. Our teams are using the available technology and we are finding that they are not on top of the latest innovations and are not applying technological innovation to our business: 29.93 percent.

c. Our teams are a mix of people who are highly technically savvy and those who are resisting technology or learning more about how to use it more effectively to do his or her job: 43.48 percent.

d. Our teams are resisting the technological innovation we are requiring to move ahead as a business, we are providing training and resources and there is still a huge resistance to embracing the change of new technologies: 9.18 percent.

The responses to this question confirm that technology is the biggest disruptor happening in business right now. The highest response was for answer c, our teams are a mix of people who are highly technically savvy and those who are resisting technology are learning more about how to use it more effectively to do their jobs, with 43.48 percent choosing this response. This was great from my point of view in that those who are resisting are learning. This is a key distinction because learning is the discovery phase of the change cycle, which is focused on learning and growing rather than on focusing on the fear of having to learn a new technology, which would be resistance. However the next highest response was answer b at 29.93 percent: our teams are using the available technology and we are finding that they are not on top of the latest innovations and are not applying technological innovation to our business. This would indicate that there is an energy-neutral approach as it relates to managing the status quo of using what they know rather than stretching to leverage technology knowledge and then using that next level knowledge to drive innovation. For those who chose this as their response, I would recommend a focused project plan on getting buy-in from all people to learn more about the technologies available, provide training on the technology, and create reward programs around innovation and creative solutions using the technology. I was very pleased to see that 17.93 percent chose answer a, and ultimately I would like to see that number rise exponentially—our teams are highly technologically savvy and are consistently on top of technological innovation and how to leverage technology to improve our business. I was also encouraged that only 9.18 percent chose answer d, our teams are resisting the technological innovation we are requiring to move ahead as a business, we are providing training and resources and there is still a huge resistance to embracing the change of new technologies. For those companies that chose answer d, I would suggest that they undergo a full change-leadership program that includes assessing where there is fear/blocks to change, providing project timelines for training and resources on leading change and all aspects of people skill development that goes with that, such as personality styles, conflict management, and so forth, and then circle it back to the technology training once there has been focus on navigating the change and providing skills and resources on adapting to and leading change.

Question 7: When it comes to the fast pace of change in your workplace what would you say the reasons are for most people to fear the changes?

Multiple Choice Answers/Responses
   a. We have a large group of people who have worked for many years in his or her jobs and they are afraid of not being able to keep up to the new technologies: 31.88 percent.

b. We have many people who have been in the previous culture which was that "time on job" meant superiority and now that our focus is on performance, not time on job, some people are afraid for their own jobs: 32.85 percent.

c. We have many younger people who are wanting change and thrive with it and they fear not learning as much as they can while they work for us: 14.01 percent.

d. We have a culture in which there has been so much change and our teams have witnessed layoffs and, rather than focus on creative solutions, they are focused on the fear of being let go: 21.26 percent.

This is an important question because it relates to the fears that our people are experiencing in relation to the fast pace of change. Often, leaders will neglect to address the reality of fear as the factor in slowing down the pace of transformation. The answers to this question confirms the fear that people have with 32.85 percent choosing b, we have many people who have been in the previous culture, which was that "time on job" meant superiority, and now that our focus is on performance, not time on job, some people are afraid for their own jobs. The shift in culture from entitlement to performance-based is a big one, and one of the biggest transformational opportunities right now for many organizations in diverse industries. The fear of losing a job is a big reason that people will balk at change rather than lead it. The focus is on self-protection rather than on the overall good of the company and the business. Change leaders need to provide the link to employees that driving transformation means increased business and increased business means higher likelihood of people having jobs. Answer d was similar to this one in that it was about fear of losing a job with 21.26 percent saying we have a culture where there has been so much change and our teams have witnessed layoffs and, rather than focus on creative solutions, they are focused on the fear of being let go. A coach approach of meeting with all individuals one-on-one to discuss fears, to provide information and resources would be a valuable approach to the fear of losing jobs. In addition, having regular large group meetings where the focus is on communicating the changes, reminding everyone of the tools and resources available, and openly being truthful about job futures is critical.

The other answer that was chosen by 31.88 percent was a, we have a large group of people who have worked for many years in their jobs and they are afraid of not being able to keep up to the new technologies. This answer would indicate that there is a large demographic of Traditionalists and boomers in the workplace and that there is an opportunity to set up hands-on technology training and reverse mentoring where a Gen Y or Gen X spends time with the traditionalists and boomers to show them how to leverage technology. I have found that many companies just expect that all technology training be learned the same way, by using an online tutorial or by watching videos. This type of learning works better for the Gen Ys and Gen X. My experience has shown that Traditionalists and boomers prefer to be shown how to do something in person because this is how they best understand difficult concepts. This also means that they may need to be shown repeatedly in order to learn a complex technology.

Providing ongoing technology training in multiple formats (web based/gaming/in class/in person/hands on) is the solution for this one.

The lowest response on this question was 14.01 percent and was answer c, we have many younger people who are wanting change and thrive with it, and they fear not learning as much as they can while they work for us. This response rate would indicate that the companies who responded with this as their answer have a larger demographic of Gen Ys and that their desire is to be in a fast-changing environment *and* they want to learn as much as they can so that they can take that knowledge elsewhere. An October 2014 *Harvard Business Review* article stated that one of the benefits of companies having employees who change jobs frequently is that it increases multisector experience. The article went on to state that the more employees that have multisector experience, the more innovation ability they bring to the companies they work for. Think of it as cross-pollination of ideas. Gen X and Y do not see having multiple jobs on his or her resume as a bad thing; rather, it is seen as having diverse experience and knowledge. This is one of the major reasons I encourage companies to teach all employees everything they can, because it ups the knowledge for all to improve current job skills and, even though they may take that knowledge elsewhere, conceivably you are hiring more multisector experience employees in return.

Question 8: What do you think needs to happen for your company overall to either continue or to be an industry leader in relation to transformation, innovation, and leaders of change?

Multiple Choice Answers/Responses
  a. We need to regroup and revisit our strategic vision, mission and values as a senior leadership team: 10.14 percent.
  b. We need to engage the entire company in the vision and take the time to meet one-on-one with every person to ensure he or she sees his or her role in the future of the company as we drive forward: 40.10 percent.

c. We need to renew our overall culture to be focused on performance, not tenure, and we need to reward and recognize those who are demonstrating transformational actions toward business growth: 34.30 percent.

d. We need to embed a new way of thinking and doing with our entire company that includes the need to be entrepreneurial thinkers and decision makers: 15.46 percent.

This question had majority responses from b and c. They are similar questions, and if we total the two together the overall percentage is 74.40 percent, a very high leaning toward the need to engage the entire company as well as renew the overall culture. Those who chose a, we need to regroup and revisit our strategic vision, mission, and values as a senior leadership team would, indicate that for those 10.14 percent there is an opportunity for the senior leadership to realign vision prior to engaging or involving the entire company. The 15.46 percent who selected d, we need to embed a new way of thinking and doing with our entire company that includes the need to be entrepreneurial thinkers and decision makers, sees the need for a complete transformational approach that would include a cultural transformation on beliefs, thoughts, and change leadership approaches as well as intense training and coaching on being "entrepreneurial" on the job.

Question 9: When it comes to your own leadership style as a change leader and a driver of transformation, what do you think is your biggest asset?

Multiple Choice Answers/Responses

a. The ability to see all the moving pieces and to value people more than processes: 22.71 percent.

b. The ability to build strategy and have the vision to execute with my team—the leadership style of providing the resources needed by my teams to do their best job possible: 22.22 percent.

c. The ability to be a very adaptable and agile thinker and to respond to other people in a way that focuses on his or her value which then influences them to want to support the vision and goals set out: 27.54 percent.

d. All of the above: 27.53 percent.

The survey respondents were pretty evenly spread out on the answers to this question. The good news from my perspective is that almost 30 percent said all of the above, which indicates a third of the respondents have highly developed change leadership skills. Those who responded with all of the above are well positioned to transform culture and continue to transform business as well.

The a, b, and c, answers are all valuable change leadership skills *and* the opportunity is to develop all areas described to be a transformational leader.

Question 10: As you look at the future workplace to the year 2020, what do you think will be the biggest change that will affect business overall?

Multiple Choice Answers/Responses

a. Technology will continue to rapidly change and we will be working with teams of people who will interface and interact with robots: 25.60 percent.

b. There will be less hierarchy and more working teams in which everyone is the leader with greater autonomy among teams and greater accountability: 25.60 percent.

c. There will be fewer task-related jobs and more projects that will be completed by both internal teams and out-sourced teams to meet specific targets and mandates: 20.77 percent.

d. The race for talent will continue, as having top performers will be even more crucial than it is today given the speed of upcoming changes: 28.02 percent.

These answers show that there is no clear winner of the predictions for the future workplace. In actuality all the answers are true. The respondents chose d, the race for talent will continue as having top performers will be even more crucial than it it's today given the speed of upcoming changes as the slightly higher choice, at 28.02 percent. Concurrent research with mine from the Future of Work Institute and other futurists such as Faith Popcorn all corroborate the findings that the future workplace will include robotics, war for talent, more project work and outsourcing, and less hierarchy.

TRANSFORMING THE WORLD, ONE PERSON AND ONE COMPANY AT A TIME

When I set out to write this book, I was the most excited I have ever been about a project. I truly feel blessed to do work I love, to do the work I love probably until I am well into my late years. I love what I do so much that it does not feel like work.

Writing this book was joyful and hard work and caused me to evaluate my skills as a transformational change leader. I asked myself constantly if I was doing what I was suggesting, and it helped me to raise my game with my clients even more than before.

I believe that we can transform the world by first focusing on transforming ourselves as individuals and then leading others to change and transform. That is the energetic focus that sustained me as I wrote this—the vision was bigger than myself. I had set a compelling vision and I embarked on the hero's journey, and yet the journey has just begun.

I would love to hear your success stories and invite you to find out more about how to be a part of a group of transformational leaders from around the world. I have a group of leaders focused on continual transformation and they are known as evolutionaries. Find out more at www.evolutionaryleadersnetwork.com.

In service and all the best to you and your efforts to master the art of change leadership and to drive transformation in a fast-paced world.

ABOUT THE AUTHOR

Cheryl Cran is an internationally known expert and highly regarded speaker and consultant on future of work, change, leadership, and transformation. Her work in creating transformational change has produced unprecedented results for the companies who work with her. Cheryl is the CEO of Evolutionary Business Solutions Inc. (www.evolutionarybusinesssolutions.com), and its parent company, Synthesis at Work Inc., a global consulting and training firm working with companies to deliver outstanding performance.

Cran's proven approach is "change leadership" and not "change management." The major differentiator between good and extraordinary companies is having leaders with the elevated skill set to lead change and transform. This includes companies with successful leaders who have the ability to lead with 20/20 vision and create the future workplace today.

Cheryl is the founder of Evolutionary Leaders Network, a vital resource and forum for professionals at all levels to help them be on the leading edge of change, leadership, and transformation strategies. The Evolutionary Leaders Network provides a mechanism for like-minded leaders to network, mentor, and learn cutting edge skills to drive transformation in the workplace with some of the top minds in business.

Cran is the author of six books and has developed specialized training programs available for delivery by license. The specialized licensed training programs that she created from her bestselling book, *101 Ways to Make Generations X, Y and Zoomers Happy at Work*, are being delivered by certified trainers throughout the world.

Cheryl has been invited as a guest lecturer at numerous colleges and universities including University of Victoria, Duke University Singapore, University of British Columbia, and Douglas College.

She has been named one of North America's top female keynote speakers and has been inducted into the Canadian Speaker Hall of Fame.

Cheryl has also presented at TEDX and has been a featured expert in many media sources including *New York Metro*, the *Financial Post*, *Entrepreneur Magazine*, *Readers Digest*, *Selling Power Magazine*, *BCBusiness* Magazine, *Malaysian Times*, *Romania News*, *The Globe and Mail*, and more.

What people are saying about Cheryl Cran:

"Cheryl Cran is not Sheryl Crow but she is a rock star nonetheless!"
 —**AT&T Leadership University–Dallas, Texas**

"We had Cheryl Cran as a keynote speaker at Duke University Singapore. The keynote was leading edge research and was truly inspiring. Cheryl's content on leadership and change was quite amazing. Our group valued her ability to connect with our culture and customize her message to the realities of working in Singapore.
 —**Duke University–NUS University Singapore**

"We had Cheryl as our keynote speaker at our annual strategic retreat for our senior leaders. Cheryl has the unique ability to 'hear' and to completely create a customized message/approach that was *exactly* what we needed. Her knowledge of technology, leadership tools, and emotional intelligence, and her ability to give us tools to leverage our skills was right on track with where we need to go as a leadership team. We have a team of highly intelligent and accomplished leaders who are quite jaded and we had one of our long-term leaders say, 'I have been coming to these for years and Cheryl was by far the most relevant and excellent leadership expert we have had to date.'

"As a leadership expert Cheryl combines research, applied knowledge, and tremendous insight that ultimately will help our leaders to perform to their next level of success."
 —**Pacific Hotel Management–San Francisco**

To find out more go to: www.cherylcran.com
www.evolutionaryleadersnetwork.com
To contact Cheryl's office: info@cherylcran.com

INDEX